Praise for *Dear Martha, WTF?*

"Unforgettable! A rare new storyteller is here to stay."

—GAIL GONZALES, Publisher, Adjunct professor,
NYU School of Professional Studies

"With riveting power and energy, Tricia LaVoice demands and finds authentic answers in her own backyard."

—NANCY MOONVES, Producer, American Actress

"LaVoice finds healing and salvation in the most charming possible form. A story rich in imagery that follows a path of letting go, forgiving, and accepting."

—HOLLY HOLMBERG BROOKS, Producer, Writer

"With heartbreak and hilarity colliding on every page, an explosion of a book asking the 'perennial' question WHY, that only Mother Nature could dare answer. A resounding new voice of transformative power and wisdom. I give it 5 stars."

—CARLENE WATKINS WEINBERGER, American Actress

"*Dear Martha, WTF?* is a story about the healing powers of friendship and aloneness in women's lives. It is a moving, insightful memoir that has the power to make readers laugh, cry, think, and change. Tricia's quirky observations permeate the book with a voice that is as hilarious as revealing. Reading this memoir is truly like journeying through life's ups and downs with your own best friend."

—JENNIFER L. HOLDER, writer and founder of Full Bloom Publications

"Captivating from start to finish, an unflinching true tale that is both provocative and poignant. A true pleasure to read."

—ELIZABETH CASH, Manhasset Book Club

"Tricia LaVoice is a soulful woman, frank and unfiltered in a really good way. Her conversations with Martha take on grief, love, the challenges of yoga, motherhood, her humorous philosophies about sex in a marriage, and other trials and tribulations of life. Her journey is one of fulfillment."

—DEBRA BRANCATO, LCSW

"Loss in all forms is an overwhelming and unpredictable journey. Author Tricia LaVoice's candor in sharing her experience is both heartbreaking and healing."

—MARGARET MCSWEENEY, author of *Aftermath: Growing in Grace through Grief*

"A must-read! *Dear Martha, WTF?* will touch many people's lives as everyone has a personal story of love and lose. Through sharing her unique experience, Tricia LaVoice demonstrates we have a choice in this hopeful, humorous read."

—PAM KING, Founder of Tyler's Warmth

DEAR MARTHA, WTF?

What I Found in   *My Search for Why*

TRICIA LaVOICE

A POST HILL PRESS BOOK

Dear Martha, WTF?
What I Found in My Search for Why
© 2018 by Tricia LaVoice
All Rights Reserved

ISBN: 978-1-68261-476-1
ISBN (eBook): 978-1-68261-477-8

Cover art by Dan Pitts
Interior design and composition by Greg Johnson/Textbook Perfect

Post Hill Press
New York · Nashville
posthillpress.com

Published in the United States of America

For Aaron

Contents

Author's Note

This book is a memoir. It reflects the author's current memories of experiences over time. While all the stories in this book are factual, some names and identifying details have been changed to guard the privacy of the individuals involved. The dialogue in the book comes from the author's recollections, and is not intended to represent word-for-word exchanges, but rather, to capture the emotion of what was shared. In all occurrences, the heart of the exchange is true.

Once she roots herself, she will take care of herself.

Her Voice

September 16, 1993

It was 4:15 p.m. Mom would be home from school by now and out of her work clothes, lying on her bed with *The New York Times* crossword puzzle, waiting for my call. I flipped on *Barney*, Olivia's favorite show, and gave her some apple slices with peanut butter. Then I jumped up on my bed, fluffed the pillows behind me, pulled my white knit throw blanket over my legs and, for the thousandth time in my life, dialed 215-295-3740.

The phone rang twice, and I heard the sweet sound of my mother's voice.

"Hello?"

"Hi, Mom, it's me. How was school?"

"Remember I told you last night I had off today, so I spent most of the day scrubbing my skin. One of the boys I work with in the special needs classroom said I smell like a banana peel. What about yours?"

"Right, right. I told you to stop wearing that fake suntan stuff. We had a good day. I dressed Olivia up in that blue dress you bought her last weekend, and we went to Rich's office to surprise him. He loved that. He was showing her off, telling everyone that she was a Ford model. I felt like an ass, but what can I say? He's a proud daddy."

1

"Did you hear about the magazine cover?"

"They photographed four babies for the December issue. We won't know who got it until the magazine is released. It's fucking ridiculous that they don't tell us."

"Tricia, please try just a little to clean up your mouth. What are you doing for dinner tonight?"

"I don't know," I sighed. "God, I hate cooking. Eating is so over-rated. Once a day, five times a week, okay, but how am I supposed to be responsible for feeding two other people three times a day *every* day? I'm baffled by this responsibility society has placed on me simply because I have a uterus."

"Luckily, your uterus lives in Manhattan," said Mom. "You can always order out. But what are you talking about, two other people? Aren't you still nursing that baby?"

"Mom, give it up. She eats food too, but I'm weaning her and I'm moving her out of the bedroom before Rich gets blue balls. It's hard, really hard, to do, but it's time."

"Blue balls?"

"Oh my God, Mother, blue balls! When a guy doesn't get laid enough, so his balls turn blue. Anyway, Rich has a business dinner tonight so I'm off the hook. I will order in and force someone from the floor to eat with me after class. Their lives are all so exciting, and I'm like the floor mom who feeds everyone now, or should I say orders in for everyone."

"Well, you have your schooling and you will be a fabulous psychologist one day."

"Oh, I'm not complaining. I love my life. And I love how we are constantly in and out of each other's apartments, and I love all the attention Olivia gets; being the floor mom is great. I'll finish school and go back to work when Olivia gets a little older, but for now I couldn't be happier. Life is good."

"I remember you cutting pictures of engagement rings out of the Sunday paper and taping them to your finger," said Mom.

"The poor guy didn't have a chance. I spotted a good catch and went for it—married in less than two years, pregnant six weeks later," I said. "Hey, you are coming up this weekend, right?"

"Yes, I thought I'd take the train up tomorrow afternoon, because I have off Friday. Daddy and I are taking Julianne to Toys "R" Us for her birthday tonight. I'll call you when I get home."

"I can't believe she's turning seven years old." I glanced at Olivia, thinking it was less than five minutes ago that my sister's sweet blue-eyed daughter was exactly that small. "I'm not letting Olivia grow up. I'm keeping her small and on my hip forever."

Mom laughed. "Okay, honey, I'll talk to you in a few hours. Enjoy your class. I love you."

On my way out a little while later, I dropped Olivia across the hall with Carol. Our apartment building was fifty-one stories high, filled with babysitters, friends, interesting people to ride the elevator with, and odd people to ponder. And our floor was the best, like the ensemble cast of a sitcom—the beautiful model, the computer nerd in geek glasses, the uptight banker, the hot young actor, the Realtor in search of love, and the newly divorced adorable platinum blond trying out her new freedom. The building was perfectly located: two blocks from Central Park, a block and a half from Lincoln Center, and right across the street from Fordham University, where I was working on my master's in Educational Psychology. St. Vincent's Church backed right up to our building. I was not a Sunday regular, but I stopped by often to light a candle and say thank you to God.

Manhattan was divine that day. The leaves were turning early with blazing orange, red, and yellow decorating Columbus Avenue. Taxicabs hustled and dodged, cutting in front of one another, beeping their horns. Pedestrians strode down the sidewalk with that Upper West Side air of late-for-my-critically-important-manicure.

My professor wasn't feeling well, so class was short, and I headed home. When the elevator doors opened to the thirty-sixth floor, I hollered, "Mommy's home."

Carol opened her door, and Olivia wobbled towards me on her fifteen-month-old legs, arms reaching out, calling, "Mommy!"

"Was she okay?" I lifted Olivia in my arms, kissing and nuzzling her, making her giggle.

"We played princess," said Carol, "and watered the plants a hundred times."

"Thank you so much. I finally started weaning her and getting her on a schedule. Hey, I'm ordering dinner. Do you want anything?"

"I'll have whatever you're getting."

"Hot roast beef sandwich, open-faced with fries, smothered in ketchup."

"Heinz ketchup."

"Of course!"

"I'll be over in ten."

I phoned the local diner on the corner of 60th Street and Tenth Avenue. The moment they heard my voice, a hot roast beef sandwich was cooking. Then, for the first time ever, I put Olivia to bed with ease. The schedule thing was new to me: setting limits, making lists, planning, organizing—these things were not my forte.

As Carol walked in, the phone rang.

"That's my mom," I said. "She's coming up tomorrow."

But it was not my mother's voice on the phone. It was my sister's.

"Tricia," she said...*Tricia*..."there's been an accident."

October something, maybe November, 1993

IT WAS 4:15 P.M. Mom should be home from school by now and out of her work clothes, lying on her bed with *The New York Times* crossword puzzle, waiting for my call. I flipped on the television and gave Olivia some pretzels. I climbed onto my bed but never got comfortable. For the thousandth time in my life, I dialed 215-295-3740.

The phone rang four times, and I heard the sweet sound of my mother's voice.

"Hi, we're not home right now, but if you would like to leave a message, we'll call you back when we get in. Have a nice day."

"Hi, Mom, it's me again. How was your day? Mine was all right. Olivia's good. I started nursing her again. She's starting to talk a lot. She asks for you all the time." Olivia chatted along to *Sesame Street* in the background.

"I need help with her, Mom. I'm too tough on her, and I'm yelling at her for making messes. I have asked for help. I tell Rich I'm too hard on her, but he says she's fine and I need to take care of myself. But I yell at her a lot, Mom, and last week I smacked her bottom. Please don't tell Daddy. He'd come unglued if he knew I touched that baby. How is Daddy? Tell him I got an A on my Cognitive Psychology test. The teacher said he would give me an extra week to study, but I took the test with the rest of the class and received one of the only As.

"Oh! I finally got my bedspread. It looks great. You were right about going with the earth tones. The white spread was beautiful but too plain. Hey, you should come visit me this weekend. We could walk to Lincoln Center or have lunch at Tavern on the Green. Or we could just lie on my bed and talk. Perfect, right? Sounds perfect to me too."

I settled in a chair by the window. The blazing autumn colors had given way to the gray overcast of early winter. Grimy salt littered the icy sidewalks. Somber rings of dirty snow circled the feet of the skeletal trees.

"Mom, I'm not doing so well. I was going to die today, but I had to

skinny, and I don't know how to stop it. I lost eleven pounds since the last time you saw me. I'm eating. I'm not throwing up. I don't have diarrhea. It's like my body is eating away at itself. I don't know if it knows what to do. Rich doesn't know what to do either."

"Mommy, juice!" Olivia chirped.

"Okay, baby. Mom, hold on. Olivia needs more juice." I laid the receiver down on the bed and went to Olivia. "Here you go, baby. Be careful."

As I picked up the phone, I heard the faint beep that meant the time allotted to leave a message had run out.

"Okay, I'm back. Where were we? I want a baby. I know. I said I was waiting until Olivia turned three, but nothing I said in the past matters. Everything is different now.

"I was pregnant for a minute last week. I did one of those home tests last Friday. I should buy stock in those home-pregnancy-test companies. God knows I've bought enough of them. I know my way around a home pregnancy test, and I could definitely see the faintest blue line. Mom, I couldn't wait to tell you. I was going to call you over the weekend, but Rich was home, and I didn't want him to hear us on the phone together. My period wasn't even due until tomorrow, so I figured that's why the line was faint. But you know what's even sadder than not being pregnant? I got my period today. I miscarried. If I hadn't done the test, I never would have known. I'm positive I saw a blue line, and then—I just cried and cried.

"No, I still won't let Rich hold me. I'll have sex to have a baby but no holding. He's a guy, Mom. He won't feel used. Okay, that was mean, but I promise you, he'll be happy with whatever he can get at this point. I know, I know, he is a wonderful man, and no one could ever love me like Rich does. I'm just telling you, I feel so disconnected. No, I'm not giving him a chance. I don't want to be held or touched by anyone right now.

"We had an awful fight last week. Rich had asked a girl in his office to watch Olivia. He felt she was doing us a big favor by helping out at the last minute because he scored tickets to this basketball game, and everyone keeps saying I need to get out and—well, I wasn't so sure of this girl, so when we got to the game, I called home, and her boyfriend was at the apartment. I called Carol and asked her to watch Olivia until I got home, and then—I don't know, things just went sideways. Rich put his face really close to mine and yelled, and I know he would never hit me, but I just reacted. I kicked him in the shin with my cowboy boot. A security guard saw and came running over. 'Hey! Hey! Do you need help, ma'am?' And Rich just stormed off. I told the guard, 'Please, leave him alone. His parents were just killed in a car accident.'

"I got a taxi, and when I got home, I put Olivia to bed and sat in the kitchen window, thirty-six floors high. You can see a lot of Manhattan. The night was cold, and the streets were covered in snow. I saw a homeless man wandering around in the church parking lot. I watched him for a long time. Swaying. Searching one trash can after another. And I felt as if I was going to die. I thought, *That homeless man and I will both die tonight.* But Olivia started crying, so I decided not to. She's nursing again. Did I mention that? I think enough time has gone by now that I'm getting it. You and Daddy are gone. I get that you're not coming back. Rich is trying so hard to be good to me, but he just doesn't get it. He's never lost anyone in his perfect little American life. Think about it, he's the only boy of four children, treated like King of the Family. His parents never fought in front of the kids. He has a successful career. No girl has broken his heart. I mean, come on! Life has been a picnic for him. He can't begin to understand the pain I'm in. The other day he asked me how many times a day I think about you and Dad. Mom, I almost died. I said, 'Rich, I don't stop thinking of them for a second.'

"I took the train home to Yardley a few weeks ago. When Olivia and I got off the train, she was looking for Daddy. She is so used to him picking us up. She was yelling, 'Papa? Papa?' I was going to die, but Liz was waiting to pick me up, so I didn't. Julianne was running around with a cast on her leg. Liz was nervous because of—you know. Julianne hit her head pretty hard that night. Don't worry, Mom, she'll be okay—or at least…better. I think I saw her smile. But you know what she did last week? She took your clothes and taped them to the wall. Liz said that the Sunday-school teacher asked the kids to draw a picture about Jesus, and Julianne drew a picture of two cars crashing.

"I went and watched Aaron play soccer while I was in town. He did real good, quickest nine-year-old on the field. He doesn't talk much anymore. Liz is trying to help him, but he just wants his grandparents.

"No. Mother, please don't tell me there's a reason for every-thing or that you're in a better place or some such bullshit. I will kick the next person who says something like that to me. I know they're trying to help. They always say they're praying for me and change the subject to make me feel better. Well, I don't want to feel better, and I'm not praying. If I can't talk to you, I'm not talking to him. I'm angry. God and I broke up. If God is so wonderful and loves me unconditionally, then he should understand. What fucking good has praying done for me? I'm sorry for the language, Mom, but what would you like me to say? 'Dear God, I have negative feelings towards you due to the grave misfortune you have placed upon me and my sisters.' My whole life I have asked for so little. My prayers were prayers of gratitude! Pardon me if I forgot to say, 'Oh, by the way, God, please don't let some asshole slam into my parents at a red light and kill them.'"

I was silent for a minute. Olivia had fallen asleep on the floor, her hands curled around her bottle, bright drops of juice still on her lips.

"Liz and Eva and I went through your things. Sorry for looking at your personal stuff, Mom. I went through your closet and smelled your clothes. They still smell like you. I really miss you, Mom. I know Daddy would be so upset if he knew Rich and I were fighting. Rich kept moaning in the middle of the night, reaching down to hold his leg. That homeless man seemed so out of it.

"It's almost Christmastime. I went into a store on Fifth Avenue yesterday, and they were playing Christmas music. I couldn't take it so I left. The city is decorated beautifully and people are happy. I don't think they know what has happened. The homeless man looked really cold. I don't think he had a coat on. I called down to the front desk and asked them to make sure he was cared for. Oh, Mom—I almost forgot. I need that noodle chili recipe. I tried to make it last night and screwed it up."

December 1993

It was 4:15 p.m. Mom should be home from school by now and out of her work clothes, lying on her bed with *The New York Times* crossword puzzle, waiting for my call. I flipped on *Barney* and gave Olivia...something. And for the thousandth time in my life, I dialed 215-295-3740.

The phone rang and rang. And then I heard an unfamiliar voice say, "The number you have reached has been disconnected and is no longer in service."

My breath hitched in my chest. I hung up and quickly redialed.

"The number you have reached has been disconnected and is no longer—"

"No, no, no...please..." I redialed, pacing the floor by the window.

"The number you have reached has been—"

"No! Please, let me talk to her! *Please*. I need to hear her voice."

I crumpled onto the bed and buried my face in my pillow so Olivia wouldn't hear my crying turn to screams. The pain suffocated me. The pillow stole my air. Olivia stirred and instinctively searched for my breast, the only form of physical contact she could rely on anymore.

"Mommy," she said, "nursies, nursies."

"*No!*" I jerked away. "No more goddamn nursies!"

Her sweet eyes widened, her lip curled, and she rolled her little body into the pillow and cried as I stumbled to the bathroom. I didn't recognize the face staring back at me from the beveled mirror. My eyes were gray. My skin hugged my bones. My expression was vacant. The urge to throw up overcame me. My stomach muscles convulsed violently until there was nothing left except the lining of my stomach and bile from my liver. I heaved until that was gone too, heaved until my head throbbed and I felt a warm stream of urine down the inside of my leg. I flushed the toilet and pulled the sleeve on my cotton T-shirt over to wipe my lips and chin, staring at the yellowish contents swirling around the bowl.

I understood then. In that moment. The world and I were forever changed. I was different. Broken. Slumped on the cold tile floor, I allowed the anger inside me to turn to rage. I looked up to the sky and said, "Fuck you. *Fuck* you. FUCK. YOU."

For a split second, I could breathe.

PART ONE

Loneliness

Twelve years later...

CHAPTER 1

Hello, Martha

I was lying on the grass in the Connecticut sun next to Martha. We were having one of our typical conversations, during which I talked my guts out and she listened.

"What if we had all the answers, Martha? I'm not talking about faith and what a book tells us to believe, I am talking cold-stone facts. Let's say God came and sat right across from you and She told you everything. She just laid it all out for you, giving you superpowers to see beyond the limitations of the human mind, to perceive existence with no beginning and no end. Let's say She had a really good explanation for suffering and tragedy, fear and hatred.

"And what if She just gave up the roadmap to peace and happiness? Would you take it and skip all the lessons of life? How differently would you live? Would you live without so much fear in your life? Would you live without judgment? Oh please, we are all judgmental. But what about those stories in your head, would you give them up? Would you speak your mind, take more risks? And what about forgiveness: do you think if you had all the answers, you would forgive others more easily?

"Oh, and what about yourself: would you forgive yourself? They say life is a journey. I hate that phrase; it makes me want to eat yogurt and chant. But would you give up the journey in order to get all the answers up front?

"Don't count on me to get the answers for you; God and I are in a fight, again! What about fear? Oh please don't tell me you have no fears. The world is riddled with fear, Martha; it competes with love as the most powerful human emotion.

"Okay, maybe you do know more about this than I am giving you credit for. What do I know about what you know? Feel free to tell me to fuck off, that needs to be an option in our relationship if we hope to have one of any value."

🌱 🌱 🌱

I AM A GENIUS at moving to a new environment and seeking out women of love and strength. I'm not sure if it is my birth order, my strong connection to femininity in general, or my desire to be like these women, but as soon as I saw her I was sure that Martha was like no one else I had ever known.

I had met her only recently, but it felt like I knew her my whole life and—more important—she knew me, she got me, and she accepted me: all of me. It was a typical morning when I opened my front door and did what I do most days: I walked. I walked through the neighborhood. Houses lined the streets, but true life was to be seen and heard amidst nature. Every day, I tried to take it in, but the voice in my head was too loud.

All my life, I had been surrounded by people—and now there was no one's voice but my own, reminding me what a loser I was for not being grateful. My own voice, telling me I deserved to be miserable and how horrible everyone else was for not understanding.

I knew what people were thinking; I took Psych 101 too. Aaron's death had unleashed the demons that had once haunted my mind before I brilliantly hid them from the light. I had come to trust life again. I had trusted God and he screwed me yet again...just when I was feeling the love, I got fucked again.

So only my own voice accompanied me on those walks, and the panic rot in my stomach, which was a reminder of everyone who was gone forever. My own voice, telling me that the actively fun life I used to hide behind was over; that was for other people to live. My parents would never show up at a school event for one of my children; that was for other families to enjoy. My nephew, a child so close to my heart, would never have the chance to figure out what life was all about; that was for other teenagers to experience. And my sister would never get to watch her child grow up; that was for other mothers to do.

My own voice, telling me that people die in my family so I'd better stay anxious, stay sick, without anyone knowing. Because if I dare to trust again, next time it may be one of my children. As I walked, my own voice was the only one I could hear, and it was screaming at me that I was lost, lost, lost.

As I headed up the driveway with this familiar pit in my stomach and twirl in my head, I felt the presence of someone watching me. But I wasn't scared; I felt almost safe. And then I spotted her, so beautiful and grand, a pillar of strength and love just sitting on the edge of our driveway as if she had been waiting for me for years.

How kindly she overlooked the children's bedrooms. Behind her was a forest, thick and thriving; in front of her was our home. She had been there from the moment we moved in, of course, but it wasn't until that moment that I found her: the most loving tree my heart could bear.

The bottom half of her was covered in ivy so that it looked like she was wearing a skirt. And her upper branches sprouted out like arms reaching to hold me. It was surreal—overwhelming—a feeling I had never experienced before; but I had the strongest sense she was a very wise old woman watching over my house, making sure my children stayed safe, making sure I would be okay. She was a Martha, I felt it.

🌳 🌳 🌳

"YOU KNOW, MARTHA, I used to say that if I could talk to my parents just once more, I would say, 'Mom and Dad, guess what? I have four babies.' I thought that would tell them everything they needed to know about how I'd moved on and time healed all wounds and I'd survived. I was whole again. Rest in peace. Good to go.

"By all practical standards, for both purpose and appearances, I did get it together. I mean, look at my life, Martha. Here I am, living in Connecticut in a beautiful house with four healthy children and a husband who loves me. I've always done everything I was supposed to do. I've always had friends. I've laughed. I've tried to help people. But I'm not whole, and I'm not sure whether peace is possible anymore. I'm alone and sad and I feel so ashamed that I feel this way.

"My parents brought us to church enough times for me to know that I was not a good Catholic girl, because I did not go religiously. Shame haunted me much of my life with no explanation other than that I was alive, a creature of God on a journey called life. During Easter of sixth grade, I stood in a circle in the middle of the church with the Janowsky family. We had all just finished confession and were praising the priest when he pointed out it was my voice he heard in 'the little black box' and I was a naughty girl. I felt that shame.

"But Martha, what could I have possibly told him? That I lied to my mother, talked behind a friend's back? What horrible sins had I committed in twelve short years of life—or at least in the month since my last confession—that I was chastised in such a way that I can recall it now? Fucker.

"Yes, Martha, I know shame, and I also know suffering. I'm not talking about pain, I'm talking about suffering: the state of being physically alive while emotionally dead. Those moments when you need to function, all the while wishing you were physically dead. Suffering: when you keep fear closest to your heart, thinking nothing bad can happen again as long as you feed the fear big bloody bites of your soul.

"My whole childhood, I got homesick, but there was always my mother's arm to run to as soon as I called for her to come get me—wherever I was. There are no arms waiting for me now. I find myself living between the latte and the chardonnay. I wake up in the morning thinking how soon I can get to Starbucks, and after I live out my caffeine buzz, I eat and drink very little, waiting for that glass of chardonnay in the evenings.

"Many times it turns into two glasses, which only adds to my self-loathing in the morning. I repeat this cycle daily, except for weekends, when I leave guilt behind.

"My kids are great; they don't seem to notice that I'm sad but the dog and my husband do. Do you see my husband going off to work every morning in that little sports car? He bought that for me, thinking it would make me happy. He tries, but I would rather drive a beaten-down VW and live in a mobile home with friends than live in this big house in the middle of nowhere.

"Martha, the kids are clueless that I'm unhappy in Connecticut. Actually, if you ask them, they may think I'm even happier than usual because they are my only focus. My sadness slows me down, which gives me more time to just sit and be present with them. But Rich notices a difference, and for the first time in my marriage, I'm not happy. I don't mean unhappy with the marriage, just unhappy with life. Oh, I have been plenty sad before but this feels different. Rich hates that I'm so unhappy—as if I have a choice.

"Life is totally different for him here. He has his best friend, and every morning he walks through the door at work and people say 'good morning' to him. The same faces every day, and he works on projects and has people kissing his ass all day long. My marriage to Rich has worked because he is a simple, easy guy who works his ass off. He doesn't have many needs, so I am able to meet his needs. I'm a tad more complicated. I need a lot of emotional intimacy and deep emotional connection. We worked because I had my mother to talk to all day long, and girlfriends. And Rich loved it—it was a girl thing to him.

"After my mother died, there was Terese and then Barbara, plus a plethora of other women friends that fulfilled the voids my marriage did not. Now, I have very little of that emotional bonding going on with friends, and Rich can't fill that void. Even if he tried, it is just not part of his DNA.

"He's not used to me being anything but the family sunshine, and when I'm not shining, he's frustrated. Sensing Rich's unhappiness is scary for me. No matter how close I am to my girlfriends, I need things to be okay with Rich and me. I always made sure he was happy with me, and I made sure he was taken care of. I'm used to him being happy with me, so I feel his frustration and unhappiness, and it makes me anxious. He is a wonderful man, my family. I can't lose him.

"Do you see my beautiful children? I know you can see right into Olivia's window from where you stand. That must be scary sometimes, as she is thirteen going on thirty. She's our oldest and only girl. I wanted to give her a sister so badly at one time, but now, I see it is perfect this way. There is no room for two girls in this family.

"That's Billy's room over there—he's eleven and quite the joker. Please keep a good eye on that one. He is always climbing and jumping. You will never see him without a ball of some sort. The two younger boys treat him like he is a king. It drives Olivia crazy. She says they should make a religion out of him.

"The room down there on the end belongs to Jack. Jack is a fabulous nine-year-old. He is different from the other kids. I hope I am doing the right thing by allowing it. He seems happy, but he is alone a lot. He's our artist and thinker. Thinkers are great as long as they don't over think. I was told a lot growing up, 'Don't think so much.' Not by my parents but by friends and then once, a therapist. Jack didn't start talking until he was three. I know my friends were worried, but I wasn't. Jack is a fabulous sculptor. One morning I picked him up at Montessori school, and the teacher grabbed me at the door and said, 'Look at him, he hasn't moved since you dropped him off this morning.' Jack was sitting in his little chair with a mound of Play-Doh in front of him that was skillfully shaped into a dinosaur. He has had a piece of clay in his hand ever since. He can make any animal you ask him to make without even looking down or looking at a picture. He even gives them buttholes, he is so into detail. We never have to buy him toys; just clay because he makes all his own creatures and toys.

"You can't see Bobby's room from here, because it's around back. He's the baby of the family, five now. He is just the sweetest little boy in the whole world. He is so friendly that I have to watch him really carefully, because he will go off with anyone. Can you help me with that? Please?

"The kids are all I have now, but they are meeting new friends and settling in here, so I need to give them that space to live their innocent lives.

"I don't know if my friends abandoned me on purpose or if life just carried on. Maybe I just used up my allotment of empathy, burned everyone out on the last round of misery. I've learned that, after a while, people don't care if you have reason to be miserable; they have their own problems and you get dumped if you don't show up with a smile on your face.

"So I feel embarrassed and ashamed—pathetic, actually—as all this begins to trickle down to my marriage. My wonderful marriage has always been my base, my core; but it feels so fragile now. Rich just doesn't know what to do with me. His happy, 'I will take care of you' wife, is miserable, and he's pissed. From his point of view, he's given me everything, worked his ass off daily to provide for me much of anything I want. But how silly for a man to think that is all I need.

"Martha, are you thinking poor Rich would be so much better off if he married someone else? I think that sometimes too. He had known me less than three years before all hell broke loose. How different his life might have been if he'd chosen a different partner.

"I worry about whether we'll make it, Martha, and I feel guilty for not being more grateful, but then I get angry at him for not getting it. I need him to sit with me and talk about his day, talk about what I'm thinking and understand my feelings. Not a chance. He comes home from work exhausted after talking all day, and what he needs is a good dinner, a back massage, and some quiet time to play chess. Of course he needs sex too, so in my misery, I'd better put on that happy face and be the sex kitten he married. I pull the 'not in the mood' card from time to time, but the price I pay for that isn't worth it. He wholeheartedly denies giving me any backlash when I say no to sex, but I feel that cloud permeating the house. I'd rather take one for the team. Keep everybody happy.

"I could turn to God, but that feels hopeless. I've given up on Catholicism. In the past, Mass brought love to my heart, a connection with the community, a sense of peace. Now it brings frustration. Bobby is the last of the children to make his Communion, so I bring him regularly to the local church. A life-sized Jesus, skin and bones, hangs over the altar to remind us of our sins. I wondered why he looked so malnourished and if he actually looked anything like the representation before us.

"I watch Bobby looking up at him as the priest speaks about Jesus dying for all of us, because we have sinned. It goes against all of my parenting beliefs; yet out of tradition and guilt and fear, I return my child to those pews week after week, and every week I spend the drive home telling him what a good person he is. My father did his best trying to drill that into me. He would say, 'You may do a bad thing from time to time, but you are always a good person.'

"Why would God make his world so beautiful and wonderful and then make his people sinners and bad? And why, Martha, would he give us this beautiful gift of life and then make us feel so guilty for having it? It's like giving your children everything they wanted for Christmas, and then—just when their little faces can't smile any longer—you nail them with how hard you had to work to pay for all of it. Sure, you want them to be appreciative and grateful, but is it necessary to remind them every time they pull the toys out, what you gave up so they could play? Is that what God wants?"

I sat up, apprehensive, and looked closely at Martha. Had I crossed the line, I wondered, and gone nuts in my loneliness and silence? But Martha stood tall and strong and seemed to say, "I understand. I will listen."

So I lay back down in the warmth of her company. "That's why I sit here and talk to you. Because I'm not crazy, Martha. I'm surviving."

CHAPTER 2

Tell It Like It Is

"We don't talk like this around here."

"What do you mean? How do you talk?" I asked.

"I mean, we just don't talk about those things."

"Well, I promise you, each and every one of you knows someone who has had plastic surgery and someone who is not circumcised," I said.

I tried to appear interested as we sipped our coffee at the local Starbucks. I had met one of the three women I was sitting with at the same Starbucks a week earlier. They were kind and polite, all dressed in Anne Taylor or maybe it was Banana Republic. I wore a floral sundress with a scoop neck. Since moving to Connecticut, I had learned to reel in my cleavage.

Moving had become part of my life. I could not remember the last time I'd lived somewhere for more than five years. It wasn't supposed to be that way. It was just the way things turned out in Rich's career. We started our family with two children in New York, then we moved to San Francisco, where I gave birth to two more, before moving to Los Angeles, where Rich put a stop to my reproducing with a simple incision. And then we moved to a small town outside of Hartford, Connecticut.

Our first summer in Connecticut went by pretty quickly. Rich was crazy busy at work and was reuniting with some colleagues he had known for years. I kept in email contact with friends.

Dear Friends,

If you are missing any socks, they are on the floor of my laundry room. Also, there are some myths I would like to debunk after living in the suburban woods:

1. A lot of sex does not bring you closer, it just gives you a yeast infection.

2. Being alone with your family all the time does not bring you closer, it makes you fight more.

3. Absence does not make the heart grow fonder, the heart doesn't grow at all when it is absent.

4. Grocery shopping in your PJs is okay as long as you don't make eye contact with anyone.

Love, Tricia

I called anyone I could get to pick up the phone. I promised my friends that I would try to make some new friends. And I tried. But not very hard.

Summer passed and I went through the motions of September, my annual month of reliving loss, because in that month both my parents and Aaron had died. It was unbearable to think a year had passed since my nephew died. I remained completely numb to my own pain as I tried as best as possible to be support for my sister Liz.

"Liz and I have always been close, Martha, but after our parents' accident we bonded in a strange, beautiful way through the suffering. We filled in the blanks our parents left, becoming more maternal with each other and with each other's children. I loved Aaron very much, but my deep mourning needs to be private. I need to be there for my sister now, and I try, Martha, I really try. I just don't feel like I'm helping. I take the train to visit her, I call her all the time, but I feel like I say the wrong things. I just don't know what to do, how to help.

"I am frozen with uncertainty, not knowing which way to move, forward or backward, to the left or to the right, in a song with no lyrics. Fear, suspicions, and doubt rob my harmony."

☼ ☼ ☼

As more time marched on, and people got busy with their own lives, I spoke with my friends less and less. I stopped sending funny emails—I didn't feel funny or sociable. When I did speak to my West Coast friends, I felt like everyone in Los Angeles had moved on with their lives, and the only person who missed me was me. I could sense them tiring of my unhappiness.

"Martha, Connecticut is beautiful. The new house is beautiful. The people are thoughtful. It's quiet and slow-paced. It's a lot like the town I grew up in. However, after so many years living in cities, I don't fit in. With the other moves, I'd started a new life as soon as I hit the ground. I was busy with babies, new schools, and hosting. But now the kids are older and do not need me in the same way. Also, I'm sick of making new friends. I had great friends in New York and then San Francisco and then Los Angeles. I'm not so sure this town is right for me or if I'm right for it.

"Rich tries; he really does. Of course, I get plenty pissed when I complain about being lonely and his buddy still shows up to play chess. But I appreciate that Rich tries to talk to me more about the little things, and that he takes me out when he wants to just rest after a tough workweek. I want to feel better, to be better, but there is no magic wand that lifts you from despair and drops you in the land of All Better.

"I don't know about trees, but people are supposed to think and do. There is a quote I learned at Sunday school one of the few times I was listening: 'The idle mind is the devil's workshop.' That's what the loneliness does to me. It makes me feel lost and crazy, miserable, the devil's workshop of wicked thoughts. I never had such darkness in my thoughts before. I'm so lost, Martha, I don't know where to turn. I don't think anyone has any idea how sad I am and how lost I feel right now. If I tell them, I know they will all say I should go to therapy, get medication. I don't feel like I want to die, but I feel like a piece of me has died.

"Martha, the gray skies, the empty house all day—fuck, the loneliness is eating me up inside. I don't even want to talk to my friends anymore, much less go live with them. I do love Rich, I love him so very much. I hate myself for being like this, for feeling this way."

That night, I took a walk under the cloudy sky. I searched for stars but they were hidden away, and I thought about my own self, how the stars were gone from my eyes. They had disappeared after my parents died, but they came back again with all the births and love. Then Aaron died, and I worried they might be gone forever to me. I studied the sky once more and felt a tad foolish. The stars were still there. You can't remove stars from the sky; you can only temporarily cover them up with clouds. I walked some more and I wished in my mind.

When I got back to the house, I sat at Martha's feet and thought about how much I loved Rich and wished I could make him understand:

In the beginning, my skin was smooth, my smile innocent, my time was yours. In the beginning your walk was swift, your campaign eager, your enthusiasm mine. In the beginning our kiss was feverish, our dreams were boundless, our love naive. The moment was tender and forever was ahead of us, so we promised it with a relationship only experienced in pleasures and ease. We took one another's hand and walked forward into life to be challenged by reality, wrapped in beauty, shaken with despair. Now we stand looking back as much as we look forward. We have been blessed and tested; we have grown together and grown apart. My skin is no longer smooth, but you do not seem to notice. The young now dominate my time, but you seem to understand. Our love is no longer naive, but it is true; our dreams have been altered, but they remain dreams, and again, I reach for your hand, asking you to walk forward with me.

🌳 🌳 🌳

"MARTHA, WTF? Why do you undress when it gets cold out?"

I wasn't judging, just curious. I had decided to stop getting undressed in front of anyone now that everything was heading south. I can hide it well with push-up bras and Spanx, but once the undergarments come off, it all goes places it never went before.

"You know a man designed this house, Martha. Who else puts a full-length mirror directly across from the shower?"

I expected the boobs that were once my favorite accessory to get grouchy, and I expected cellulite to find a home on my backside, but I did not expect the pouch. You know, the pouch, that area between your belly button and your pubic bone that has come out of nowhere with a mission to destroy any sexy feelings you may still have about yourself. It's like the perfect middle child that rebels for not getting enough attention and now burns the house down. I agree, I never threw that area of my body much love; there were so many other body parts that needed lotion, massage, washing, and grooming. I have apologized many times for all the nights I squeezed her into control-top panties and for not appreciating her good behavior when she laid tight and flat. I've apologized for the abuse she took those last months of pregnancy when I neglected to feed her vitamin E or cocoa butter; but she remains unruly, leaving me to shop for big tops and get my own hotel room.

This morning, I found my way to the bathroom, avoiding the mirror until my face woke up. I flushed the pee I had not flushed before, in the middle of the night, before sitting down on a cold toilet seat looking at my vanity. A plethora of goods graced my countertop: hair products to keep my hair from falling out, more products to make my eyelashes grow. Creams for morning, night, and in between: lip cream, eyelid cream, neck cream, stretchmark cream, and so on.

Until a month ago, my nightly ritual consisted of nothing more than a splash of water, but things were moving fast in the wrong direction, so I took action. Also, the astute sales rep at the beauty-supply store sensed I was hungover and took total advantage of my vulnerability, telling me I had the worst skin she had ever seen on a pretty face. How could I not buy everything she suggested? She called me pretty.

Even though Rich and I may not be at our best right now, still he makes me feel beautiful and tells me so often, but let's face it, he is not that observant. I had braces for two days before I needed to point them out to him and, a week after I had my eyelids lifted, he questioned whether I had both eyes done. A friend asked me to send her a picture, so I dolled up one eye with some mascara and shadow before sending off a text. Rich had just returned home after I photographed myself. He asked, "Did you only have one eye done?"

I replied, "Yes, it was all we could afford, but I was hoping to get the other one done in the next year."

I watched his brain twist as he tried to comprehend this before explaining the magic of makeup. But he wouldn't care if I'd had only one eye done. Whether he believes what he is saying or not, he makes me feel pretty and appreciated.

"Yes, Martha, I had plastic surgery. Three things I promised myself I would never let fall were my eyes, my boobs, and my vagina. As long as good fortune allows, I'm lifting them as they drop. I like to tell people that early in a friendship, just in case I run into that one special being who has not sinned and wants to cast a stone.

"Yes, Martha, I said 'vagina.' Not for me, but for the grandchildren. You see, men need sex. It is the glue to the marriage, and if I want to keep the marriage together long enough that the grandchildren have a warm home to visit, I need to keep the sex going. So if the vagina falls, I'm lifting it too.

"Aren't you so glad you are a tree? But wait, do you ever get pissed that you weren't born a palm tree so you could live in Florida all year? Just think about it, no cold or snow, just beaches and sun. But those palm trees get hit with some pretty bad hurricanes. In the end, everyone gets their ass kicked one way or another in this thing we call life."

🌳 🌳 🌳

I FELT LIKE NO ONE understood my unhappiness, so I got good at hiding my unhappiness. I was cheerful when I was with the kids, and Rich and I started pretending when I spoke to friends. I retreated. I found local hiking trails and walked a lot and just thought and thought. It's a different experience than any I have ever known. After my parents' death, I was able to surround myself with people and create life. Society embraced my mourning and allowed it. Rich and I were young with a lot of life ahead of us. Now, Rich travels a lot and works long, hard days. When he comes home at night, he needs my love and support. My sister Eva is struggling and my sister Liz, well, I can't bear the pain she must be in. My friends must be exhausted by all my tragedies, and my children don't deserve to see their mother's pain. This time I'm all alone and lost.

"I know loss, Martha. I thought I had come to grips with it. But now, here I am, facing a new monster called loneliness. Loneliness is a powerful, ugly force that strips you of all your defense mechanisms, leaving you vulnerable and raw, exposing the deepest, darkest thoughts you so carefully buried away. I thought I was emotionally strong and balanced, healed and healthy, but loneliness made sure I knew the truth: that I could not bear another loss. Aaron's death destroyed me, again, as if I never healed from the last tragedy.

"What happened to us, Martha? We were a good family, my mom and dad and we three girls: Liz, Eva, and me. We were a normal middle-class American family with futures and dreams. We were not hurting anyone or doing anything wrong. Sure, we had our share of issues, but what happened to us and why? I feel punished and always anticipate horror every time the phone rings. Because one night, when we were all going about our lives, the phone rang, and I became one of those stories you read in the paper.

CHAPTER 3

Mothers, Mothering, and Motherhood

My mother and I are lying on her bed. Olivia is four months old and lies in between us. I have just returned from dinner with two friends, both of whom lost a parent to cancer. One lost her mother twenty years ago; the other lost her father five months ago.

"It was so sad, Mom, I can't even tell you. Monica said even though her mother died twenty years ago, it feels like she is still just away on vacation."

"Oh, that poor child," my mother says.

"I just can't begin to imagine," I say, choking on my tears. The thought of ever losing my mother is unfathomable. I look down at my baby, trying to hide my tears, and I hold one finger out to her. Olivia immediately grabs on. My mother reaches over and cups her hand to my face.

Then, just a year later, I'm walking with my baby and mother down the streets of Manhattan. I am complete. My mother's train leaves in forty-five minutes; she hails a cab. We are standing in front of Lincoln Center. I kiss her goodbye and ask her to come back the following weekend. She hugs me and kisses the side of my face not once but twice. She takes Olivia from my arms and kisses her.

"Grandma will be back in a few days to see you, my precious baby," she says.

She hands Olivia back to me, but the baby reaches out to go with her.

"It's okay, sweetheart, Grandma is coming back soon."

My mother looks to me and smiles. The wind is blowing her soft brown hair in front of her face. She laughs as she pulls a piece from her mouth. She climbs into the back of the cab and waves goodbye as the driver pulls away from the curb. She is happy, she is beautiful, she is alive.

And I will never see her again.

🌱 🌱 🌱

"IS LOSING YOUR MOTHER part of the circle of life, Martha? Think about it: if you don't lose your mother, your mother is tasked with the far more devastating loss of her child, and you would never wish that on her. So you know it'll happen, but you're never prepared, regardless of age. We shut our minds to this fact. So many women come to me when they lose their mom, because they know I understand, and they all seem to be suffering immensely, almost in a state of depression, even women much older than me who lose their mothers when they're elderly.

"And you know what's even sadder, Martha? The woman who is not shattered by her mother's death because she never knew a mother's deep love. One way or another, we all suffer pain when losing our mothers."

My mom would go so far as to buy real baby food for my dolls and let me come home from school at lunchtime to feed them. There would always be music playing and a grilled cheese waiting. On the days I liked what the cafeteria was serving, I would stay at school and she would promise to feed my babies. It was the little things— the icing on the cake that made my childhood so sweet, and her, the best mommy in the world to me.

She would lay towels around me on the bed and floor so I never had to get out of bed if I was throwing up—she just kept changing out the towels instead of bringing me into the toilet. I thought about how she would always give me this horrible-tasting medicine called paregoric for every aliment, and how she stayed with me all night rubbing my back softly and humming, nothing in particular, just humming.

In one very vivid memory, I am young and I am hungry.

"Can I eat it now?" I ask.

"No, it's still too hot."

I sit patiently waiting for my soup to cool down. Again, I impatiently ask, "Can I eat it now?"

My mother walks over to the table and bends down to my bowl. As her lips meet with the broth of the soup she jerks back and drops the spoon. I just watch.

"Can I eat it now?"

"Give it a few more minutes. Okay?"

I sit quietly and watch as she goes to the freezer and removes a piece of ice from the tray and turns away from me.

"Are you okay, Mommy?"

"I'm fine, baby."

As she walks out from the room I can see she is holding the ice to her lip. I continue to sit quietly waiting for my soup to cool down.

I loved everything about my mother. I loved how she wore white often and how she gave her cars names like Betsy and Marilyn. I loved the way she smelled and the way she always knew what I was thinking. I loved sitting next to her going on shopping trips to Pomeroy's and J. C. Penny. I loved the way I could get her to do anything I wanted if I cried and how she never yelled at me. I loved how she let me dress in her clothes, even her best dresses, and how she always had a project going on. I loved everything about her. I simply loved her.

One of my favorite things to do was stand in front of the long mirror in my mother's room and look at myself while she was getting ready to go out somewhere.

"I can see a whole bunch of me if I stand like this in front of the mirror." I am about eight years old.

"Now, there's that much more of you for me to love," my mother said.

"Come stand with me," I begged.

"Tricia, I can't. I'm late already!"

"Please!"

"Okay, real quick."

Dionne Warwick is singing "What the World Needs Now" in the background. My mother's hoop earrings swing back and forth as she moves her head and sings along. I reach out and feel the suede of her miniskirt. Tonight she looks super pretty and cool. My father must be taking her somewhere special.

"Kiss the mirror," I instruct.

"I will ruin my lipstick."

"Look, I can kiss it perfect." I lean over and kiss the mirror, leaving a perfect imprint of my mother's pink lipstick on the mirror.

"Hey, were you in my stuff again?"

"Yep, but look how good I made the kiss."

She leans over to the mirror and kisses my kiss. I giggle; she is my world.

❦ ❦ ❦

I KNEW A WOMAN WHO was one of four growing up. She told me she never got enough attention and resented her parents for it. She also said that her mother would lie in bed alone with each one of her children every night, and how special that time was for her. I never forgot that conversation, and I made every effort to give each of my children special moments of my undivided attention before bedtime. We would talk about their day, their feelings, and their fears. I treasured these moments.

"Good mothers are always beating themselves up, Martha. That's how they stay good mothers. But it is not necessary, and it is damaging. I feel so bad that Olivia's early years got disturbed by my parent's accident. She was the only one constantly at my side those first couple of years after the accident. She is a clingy child, the touchy-feely type. Maybe the Latin, Spanish blood that is in my black Irish got in her bloodstream. Maybe I nursed her too long. But I am not the physically mushy type. I can't dance either. If the accident hadn't occurred, I would laugh while complaining that she was trying to get back in the uterus; but instead, I worried that I wasn't giving her enough physical love. I nursed the child until she was two, and I have numerous pictures of me holding her and kissing her; yet I remember feeling like I closed up after the accident, like the accident changed me, when I can see now it opened me up."

But I was forced to go through the highs of motherly love and the lows of fearing loss when Billy was born. He is William Patrick, William for my father and Patrick for my mother, whose name was Patricia.

His birth was much easier. It was like my uterus was a cornfield and Olivia had plowed the way so Billy just shot out. I remember he lay naked under the heating lamps with his knees pulled up at his sides. I was thinking he looked like a chicken—not a chicken you would want to eat, a chicken you would send back because there was not enough meat on the bones. He was so tiny, so fragile, and so perfect. The nurse bundled him up and laid him in my arms. He looked up at me with beautiful blue eyes, and I instantly fell in love. The light forced him to squint, displaying his fabulous dimples. He made a sweet sound that made him all the more adorable. But the doctor was concerned.

"I'm going to call a pediatrician down to check him out. Don't worry, he'll be okay," she said as she took him from my arms and returned him to the heating lamp.

Two minutes later, our brand-new baby was surrounded by a team of doctors and then brought to the ICU. He had swallowed amniotic fluid, which filled his lungs. Rich went off with the baby, and I was moved to my room, feeling empty and guarded. My parents had died only a year earlier. I was totally incapable of trusting life and believing that "things will be okay." I had no emotional reserve for that.

Finally, an attractive middle-aged doctor entered my room. She was standing at the foot of my bed, and I could see she had lost her left arm from the elbow down. She began to speak but everything was so surreal: "Your baby is going to be okay. We need to keep him in the ICU now. I'll come back in the morning and check on him."

I wondered how she lost her arm. I wondered if life was difficult for her. I stayed guarded and protected. I will not love him, I will not feel, and I will not hurt.

"I know tragedy, so please be honest with me. I can handle it," I said, and then I started to sob. "My parents were killed in a car accident a year ago, both at the same time. They were just waiting for the light to change, that's all. I know death. So just tell me if the baby is going to die. Just tell me the truth."

"Your baby is going to be okay. I promise you."

Her words meant nothing to me. I realized no one's words meant anything to me. I turned my head and stared at the blank wall. She stood silent for a moment and then gave me my privacy. Rich stayed by my side until visiting hours were over. Liz brought Olivia in for a short visit. We all tried to stay calm, but they shared my lack of trust in fate. We had lost our false sense of security when the world we knew was taken away in a single moment.

I tossed and turned all night and finally fell asleep around 4:00 a.m. In a dream, I was nestled in the back seat of my mother's white 1969 Karmann Ghia. My short, hairy legs barely stretched across the light brown leather seat. My childhood best friend, Janie, sat shyly next to me, intrigued by my mother.

"Okay, Mommy, I'm closing them now. Go," I hollered from the back seat. I looked to my friend. "Janie, close your eyes and try to guess where we are."

This was one of several games I would play with my mother: me closing my eyes on the way home from a night out, while she would drive around our neighborhood and try to keep me guessing as to where we were.

She was perfect in every way and the most beautiful woman my seven-year-old self had ever laid eyes on. Everything I did revolved around her.

"Okay, where are we now?" she asked as I felt the car take a swift turn to the right and then make a complete circle around again and again.

"The church parking lot," I screamed with excitement. I knew it was the only place near my home where she could do doughnuts.

"You peeked."

"I did not. Go again. Try and fool us again," I blurted out.

Janie sat quietly as our charade carried on. Then, all of a sudden, I heard a loud screeching noise coming toward us, louder and louder. My heart started pounding, my legs went numb, and I said, "He's going to kill us!" Now it was my father driving the car and my mother was seated in the passenger seat, perfectly still facing forward. Suddenly, I was plunged deep down underwater. It was dark and cold, freezing cold. I tried to scream, "Mommy, help me!" but water filled my lungs.

I was awakened by the sense of a presence in the room. A small amount of sunrise crept through my window. I could see the doctor holding the nub of her left arm with the palm of her right hand.

"I didn't want to turn on the light, but I wanted to see you as soon as possible."

She stepped closer to my bed. "I went first thing to check on your baby. He's doing wonderfully. I'll bring him to you whenever you are ready."

"May I have him now, please?"

"I'll be right back."

🌱 🌱 🌱

I'M SITTING WITH MY FRIENDS watching the Super Bowl. The Philadelphia Eagles have not made it to the finals since 1980. We are all so excited. A car commercial comes on the television. Everyone stops and watches. The car speeds down the test drive and smashes again and again into the wall. The test dummies' heads slam forward and back again, *baboom!* Someone yells out, "Tricia! Isn't that your mom and dad?"

I woke in a sweat and got out of bed to check on the kids, who were all still peacefully sleeping. It was a rainy morning, so I gathered everyone's school clothes and threw them in the dryer for ten minutes so they would be nice and warm to put on. I thought about all the little things like this that my mother had done for me and how important it was that she taught me to do these things for my children.

I will never understand why we need to be so tough on ourselves and each other. Mothers can be the worst about judging one another, and I was no exception. I remember going to hear Hillary Clinton speak after she wrote her book *It Takes a Village*. I was younger and more arrogant at the time. Bobby hadn't been born yet. But I remember thinking to myself, *What is a working mother of one going to teach me about motherhood?* When I reflect on that now, I embarrass myself with my ignorance. Hillary was amazing, and her wisdom and insight into mothering taught me plenty that night. However, she knocked me off my feet when she said, "We women need to be more respectful of each other and the choices we make; we working women need to show stay-at-home mothers respect for their decisions." I was floored. I thought it was we stay-at-home mothers who had to show the working mothers respect.

Wow, who would have thought we all need to just mind our own business and respect one another's choices all around? I thought about that on my walk that morning quite a bit. I looked to Mother Nature for answers, questions, and insights; all I seemed to find was harmony. Everyone was just doing his or her job, allowing others to do theirs. The trees were quietly blowing in the breeze as birds flew in and out of their branches. The creek rippled over the stones, making beautiful sounds. Everything in nature just seemed to go about its business without judgment or concern for one another, while working together and creating paradise.

I thought more about the mothers in my life and how wonderfully supportive we were of one another also. I don't think any of us could do it alone. And that is why Hillary Clinton's book title was so fitting—it does take a village. I needed a village even more, without the support of grandparents, and I was so appreciative of mine. The memories inspired me to write a wish:

> *There is a well where the children go to quench their infinite thirst—their thirst for love and safety, patience, and acceptance—their endless need for confidence, reassurance, direction, trust, and respect. This well I speak of I call "you." A hole below the surface of the earth or a spring bursting with purity; no matter what you call it, it is you that is responsible for gathering the strength to quench the boundless thirst of your young. Some days, your water overflows with abundance, yet on other days, your well runs dry. Like the water that sustains their young bodies, the water from your well is essential to their being. There are no days off and the children, young and old, are not yet understanding or required to replenish what they take. So where do you go, what do you do when the depth and quality of your well water runs short? Thankfully, wells are meant to be shared by all in the village. When you tire, let your children come to my well. When I tire, welcome my children to yours, and for those in need, together, we can serve all. For you, I wish the village well.*

🌱 🌱 🌱

"MOM, HERO HAS A DINGLEBERRY," Jack yelled as he ran out the door to catch the bus. I had been up late the night before, so Rich had offered to get the kids to school for me. I climbed out of my bed feeling older than I thought I was. As I entered the bathroom, Olivia came running in to give me a kiss goodbye.

"Mom, Hero has a dingleberry, and the house downstairs smells," she said as she ran in and out so quickly I could not see her skirt. Recently the dean of students had given Olivia her very own special measuring stick to check the length of her skirt above her knees.

Rich walked in the bathroom. "Good morning. The dog."

"Yes, I know; the dog has a dingleberry. I will deal with it. Why is the dog's dingleberry my responsibility anyway?"

Rich kissed me goodbye and left the room without answering. The role of a stay-at-home housewife is such a luxury, but it does come with its cons. No matter how hard I worked, I would have to accept that many people, even those close to me, thought my life consisted of making lunches and getting my nails done. And when the kids were young and I had help, I know people thought I did even less. But the funny thing is that almost every other job out there came with helpers. Rich had a team of support at the office, from people who answered his phone to sales people moving the product. Doctors' offices were full of assistants, and mechanics had apprentices. Every job came with assistants to help the boss be more productive and get more done; but when a housewife had help, she was considered lazy and spoiled.

I fought this for a while until I finally came to a place where I did not need anyone to "get it" or need anyone to appreciate how hard I worked for my family. I knew my priorities, and I knew what I did. That, finally, was all that truly mattered.

Yes, this includes being obsessed with the laundry, but that is because it constantly outwits me. Once it is all done there is more waiting to be done; I never ever win with it. In the past, I had more help with the household stuff. Since moving to Connecticut I was slow to find help; the repercussion being, I do all the wash. I walked into the laundry room and opened the dryer to a full load of nothing but Rich's and my underwear. I wasn't sure when I got weird about washing underwear with other clothes. While I care little about much except my children picking spouses I can handle on Christmas Eve, I am officially anal-retentive about keeping anal-protective clothing away from all other garments. Plus, I like throwing only his underwear and mine in the machine together; it feels like sex via osmosis, although Rich rejects this outright.

Once, I was running around the house like a crazy lady, trying to get all of us out the door for the plane to Los Angeles and doing a wash at the same time. At the airport I got randomly selected to have my hands checked for bombing chemicals. Yep, you got it, fricking laundry detergent and bleach are all part of the potion! They emptied my bags and tested it all for chemicals and then led me into this tiny room with no windows and shut the door. One woman stood at the door while the other explained to me how she was going to pat me down. It freaked me out, so I suggested I just remove my clothes and she could look verses touch. She passed. When she finished feeling me up, I thought I should ask her to share a cigarette.

🌱 🌱 🌱

"MARTHA, OUR LIVES are a lot alike, except for the fact that you don't move from the same spot you have been standing in for a hundred years. I'm not judging you; a lot of humans like to stay put and some of us like to move around. You don't have that choice, but maybe you trees have some way of seeing all over the world just from your spot," I said to Martha as I sat on my jacket underneath her so as not to get wet from the morning dew.

"I know you have your tough winters before your amazing springs. When it comes to hardships and persevering, we humans have them too. When my parents were killed I did not know many people who had suffered tragedies. Now that I am older, I have witnessed many who have experienced horrific tragedies—parents, siblings, spouses, and the unthinkable, children.

"There are many different kinds of losses in human life that tear our worlds apart. Some come very quietly, like turning forty-five and realizing you may never have that baby you always wished for or finding yourself divorced and alone during the holidays while your kids spend the day with someone else. Some people struggle with drugs and alcohol their whole lives while others may battle their weight or health issues. Everyone experiences hardship and loss in one way or another.

"Martha, no matter how many people are around, no matter how much you are loved, it seems like we have to handle many things alone, but I get confused. Think of the sequoias—aren't they the biggest trees in the world or at least in northern America? I remember being so in awe when hearing how the sequoias wrap their roots around one another to gain their strength. That's pretty amazing that a tree could stand more than 300 feet tall by the strength of another tree. That's how I live, with the help of those around me, so being alone so much is fucking with me.

"I don't know if you realize how much people help one another. I don't know where I would be if it were not for Terese and Barbara. My friend Leeza calls them 'she-roes,' get it? Female heroes!

"After the accident, every time I took the New Jersey Transit from Penn Station to Trenton, I searched for my father in the crowd. It takes time to adjust to death. My brain, my eyes expected to find my father waiting for me as he had for years. I couldn't just shut it off. Part of me wanted to escape, to run and never stop. Another part of me wanted to curl up in a fetal position and lie on the curb for eternity. But I did not have these options. I had a life, a husband and child; I had responsibilities. Therefore, I had to confront the pain, show up for life, and pull myself up and out of the hole I had fallen into. But I couldn't do it alone; I needed the help of others before I could help myself.

"In San Francisco, there was Terese."

PART TWO

COMPASSION

*In all my searching, looking for a way to confirm
God, the only open path I could find was the
shared depth of human suffering.*

CHAPTER 4

Terese's Tenderness

In 1995, Rich took a position managing the San Francisco branch of a brokerage house. For a while, I had remained in New York City with Olivia, who was three years old; Billy, who was one; and a baby on the way, while Rich house-hunted.

I was glad that Rich had a job that excited him, but I was not looking forward to the transition. I did not want to leave my two sisters and their families—plus all the support of my incredible friends. I did not want to surrender my city-life conveniences and adjust to the role of a suburban housewife. Once I moved to California, I could no longer pick up the phone morning, noon, or night and order whatever I craved. And I ordered out a lot. After the typical Mommy and Daddy, Olivia's next spoken word was "cani." Her first full sentence was, "Call the man for my eggs."

If only Rich had married a woman who had wanted just one child, or one who went off to work in the morning and brought home a paycheck, a woman who would not spend the rest of her life grieving and healing...if we could have predicted the future, would he have run for his life? I didn't know for certain, but I don't think so. What I did know was that his devotion to our children, and to me, was and is endless. And that I could not imagine my life with any other man. He is my love, my rock, my family.

"Hi, honey. How's the love of my life?" he asked from California, in the voice that told me other people were listening. "Honey, I'm having dinner at Terese Payne's home. You would love it. The walls in her library were shipped all the way from France."

"What?" I replied. I was in no mood. It was amazing to me: before I had a husband and children, I do not think the word "bitch" would have been an adjective used to describe me. However, right now it fit. "Rich, I don't care about some rich lady's stupid-ass French walls." Terese Payne had recently stepped down from the job that Rich had taken due to a chronic illness. She was one of the most successful female brokers on Wall Street and reportedly stopped at nothing to get what she wanted.

"I'm too busy puking and changing diapers. When are you coming home?"

I was five months pregnant with Jack when Olivia and Billy and I joined Rich in Marin County, a small, beautiful part of the country located across the Golden Gate Bridge from San Francisco. We rented a sprawling contemporary overlooking the San Francisco Bay and skyline. The house was L-shaped with floor-to-ceiling windows in every room. The yard was crowded with eucalyptus trees, and we were bombarded with sounds of nature, sounds foreign to city dwellers. At night, instead of bolting the three locks that protected the only entrance in and out of our apartment, I spent fifteen minutes making sure the house was all locked up and that I was operating the alarm system correctly. Sure, the community appeared very safe, and the neighbors stopped by to welcome us. But since the accident, I had never truly relaxed.

Every morning, Rich left the house around 5:30 a.m. I didn't tell him, but I was scared of my own shadow and never rested once he left. A six-thousand-square-foot home with a guesthouse was too big an adjustment from our tiny, two-bedroom, neighbor-saturated Manhattan apartment. I felt scared and vulnerable.

One morning about two weeks after we moved in, Marin County was hit with a big storm. It was raining hard, but it was the winds blowing against the house that got me out of bed to collect Billy and Olivia. As I reached their rooms, I found them both peacefully sleeping in the comfort of their warm beds. I swung one over each shoulder and struggled my way down the long hall, my heart pounding as the trees banged up against the endless windows that lined the home. I lugged Billy and Olivia down one set of stairs and then another to my room without waking them. I climbed in bed and snuggled us under my down comforter, the rain pounding the rooftop, the sky dark and angry, and waited. Suddenly the piercing sounds of the house alarm alerted me to an intruder: the nightmare I had imagined as soon as we moved. I grabbed my sleeping children by their arms, dragging them across the plush white carpet onto the cold tile of the bathroom floor. The alarm rang so loud, I could barely think. My mind raced, *They are in the house, Tricia—two, maybe three of them. They have ski masks on, and they know you're here.* I locked the door securing us inside. The children looked bewildered, but didn't cry or question me.

"Get in there!" I pushed them through another door that separated the toilet from the rest of the bathroom and secured the lock. We sat in the three-by-three-foot space covering our ears as the alarm echoed throughout the walls. Fear ran through my veins; a narrow window, long in length, built for ventilation purposes, appeared to be my only option to save my children. Risking the child growing inside of me, I squeezed my tender body right through the window. The cold rain soaked my peach silk nightgown, covering my body in goose bumps, as my bare feet searched for the ground. I dropped about three feet into a bush, which broke my fall.

Billy and Olivia jumped into my arms, and with them resting on my hips, I ran barefoot towards the black iron gate at the foot of the property, petrified that the intruders were watching and would get us before we could make it to safety. My feet were moving in slow motion. I made it through the gate and up the hill to our neighbor's home. I'd met him only once, when we moved in. He'd visited and suggested we stop by if we ever needed anything. Rich told me he was a well-known author.

I hit the button on their intercom and again and again until, finally, a sleepy voice spoke.

"Hello?"

"Dr. Grey! Hi, it's Tricia from next door. My alarm went off!" I said in a panic.

"Oh. Okay. I'll come over and check it out."

Check it out! I thought. *Why don't you lock us in and wait for the police to come?*

Dr. Grey came out in his robe into the pouring rain. The vision of my drenched silk nightie clinging to my erect breasts and round belly while my two babies clung to my side like rain-soaked monkeys must have been an eye-opening sight at 7:30 a.m.

Immediately, my neighbor began to console us. "Please, come get dry," he said, signaling back towards his home. "I'm sure you were frightened. Alarms sometimes go off here in Marin when there is a storm. The wind blows so hard against the windows that it sets them off."

I looked down at the sight of myself, too shaken to feel embarrassed. "You're kidding."

"I'm sure it was just the wind," he reassured me.

Minutes later, a young police officer joined us and informed me that they had responded to nine false alarms that morning before coming out to our home.

"Was I the only one who jumped out the window and woke up my neighbor?" I asked, realizing how incredibly silly I must appear.

"Well, yes, you were. Where did you say you were from?" he politely asked.

"Manhattan. We just moved from Manhattan," I admitted, while I thought: *Men are from Mars, women are from Venus, and your neighbor is from Uranus.*

🌳 🌳 🌳

ONE SATURDAY EVENING a couple of months later, we were having a dinner party for some of Rich's clients. One of the guests had an inquisitive mind. She noticed two paintings in our living room. They were both painted by my mother. My father had surprised her once with art supplies; and, from that moment on, her passion for oil painting had blossomed. She painted for me a beautiful picture of a young woman leaning against a piano that I had seen in a gallery. I asked if she would paint a second copy for me, only much larger. I had planned to hang them side by side. She had almost finished the second painting before being killed—but she didn't finish the face. I hung the two paintings anyway: one small and perfect, one large and faceless. Most people who saw the unfinished painting asked about it. I was in the kitchen trying to be a good corporate wife, and I could hear Rich in the other room.

"Tricia's mom was an artist. She painted them for Tricia."

"Why didn't she finish this one? Or is it supposed to be that way?"

"Actually, she died before she could finish it."

"How sad. How did she die?"

"She was killed in a car accident, along with Tricia's father."

"Oh, that's tragic. What killed them?" she pried.

The conversation played in my head like background music. I had heard it all a million times. I got a tray from under the counter and poured some cocktail sauce into a glass bowl.

"They were in a car accident," Rich tried again.

"I understand that; however, do you know what killed them?"

Rich took a moment; I moved closer to the door to hear what he was saying. "The driver who hit them was going very fast," he said quietly. Then he added, "Both her mother and father died of internal injuries. Their necks were broken."

Bam! Fuck! Fuck! Slam! I never knew this. The light is red, the car is stopped, and they are alive and healthy. *Bam! Bam! Bam!* Their necks thrash forward, then back again. Now their necks are broken.

I walked back over to the counter and picked up the tray of food I had put together. I took a deep breath, smiled like the First Lady, and left the kitchen. "Would anyone like some shrimp cocktail?"

As far as I had understood, there had been no blood at the scene of my parents' death. I am glad there was no blood; and if there had been, I believe I would have wanted to thank the man or woman who had to clean it. I think about stuff like this, and I expect most people who lose someone tragically do as well. I assume relentless thinking is all part of the suffering. From the day they died it was important—or should I say, it was vital—that my mind replay the point of death over and over. My mind was conditioned to expect and trust that my parents were well, and I could not accept all at once that they were gone. So I replayed the details of their exit. And now I had horrifying new elements to include.

Once our guests had left, Rich and I checked on the children and then sat together under the stars. He was happy with how the night had gone and appreciative of my cooking efforts. We talked about trivial things, like what we planned to do the next day, and we discussed more important things, like how he thought his new hire was doing at the office.

We talked, and all along I had thoughts of their necks breaking, but I never mentioned it to Rich. We were enjoying the evening together like all the other married couples out there, and the last thing I wanted to do was let him know I had overheard him.

The last thing that this man deserved was any guilt over making me sad.

🌳 🌳 🌳

RICH KNEW WE WERE HAVING a boy, but no one else knew. Well, he said he told Billy but as Billy was one year old, I'm pretty positive he didn't tell anyone. I got to hold the babies inside of me, so I wanted Rich to have something special that was only his. When Jack was born, Billy was eighteen months and Olivia had just turned four. She was at my side for most of the birth. Rich was accustomed to what my father would call "Tricia's harebrained ideas," so he did not argue with me about having Olivia with us in the delivery room, but not all those present shared his sentiments.

"I really think she is too young," said one of the nurses. She'd wisely waited for me to be getting my epidural before giving her opinion. "Yesterday, a five-year-old went running out of here crying."

"Tell me something," I said as the doctor inserted a nine-inch needle into my spine, "did they bring the child in at the end?"

"Yes, her aunt brought her when the mother was ready to give birth."

"That was their mistake. You can't just walk a child into it at the last minute. Olivia has been here for eight hours. She's used to the sounds, the nurses, the doctors, seeing me wired up. She's had plenty of time to adjust to it all; plus, we practiced at home a bunch."

The doctor looked at the nurse and said, "Please, let her rest."

Olivia stood next to me and held my hands until the baby's head started to crown. I tried to keep my sound effects to a minimum, until the urge to push overwhelmed me and out came the animal sounds. "*Ahhh!*" Olivia left my side, I rushed to reassure her.

"Olivia, I'm okay."

"I know, Mommy, but I can't see." She practically climbed on the doctor's lap as she positioned herself front and center. As Jack left the birth canal and entered the world, Olivia witnessed it firsthand. She never left his side while the nurse cared for him, and then she held out her arms to be the first to hold baby Jack.

🌱 🌱 🌱

WITH THREE CHILDREN, I had no time to brood on dark thoughts; or at least, my brooding time was limited. The children brought untold happiness into our lives. I spent my days picking up toys, nursing, and going to the park. We began settling into a routine; then one Saturday, Rich and I were invited to a big wedding.

I was looking forward to the wedding and getting out of sweats and playing grown-up, but even more so when Rich informed me that Terese Payne, the woman he'd replaced, would be there. I had heard so many stories of how tough she was: she ran the office like a general and if you stepped out of line, she kicked you right back in. In my mind, she was Cruella de Vil, and the mere sound of her heels walking the halls inspired fear and attention.

The wedding itself was a beautiful garden ceremony. For the reception, we were all escorted to a huge tent that was perfectly decorated in white linen and daisies. I spotted a stern-looking woman, tall, with broad shoulders, a square jawline, and short, dark hair. I could hear her husky laugh from where I stood, and I thought, "Yes."

I wandered over and introduced myself—only to find this was not Terese.

As I continued to scan the crowd for a woman wearing puppies for a coat, I was struck by the sight of a beautiful woman standing alone, next to a pillar, near the back wall. She had the poise and elegance of Grace Kelly and the style of Jackie O. I guessed she was in her mid-forties, petite, with pale and smooth skin, and soft, shoulder-length brown hair. She looked so familiar...then she smiled and I caught the sparkle of her blue eyes. My heart sank and my stomach turned. She had the face of my mother.

I carefully approached her. "Hello, I'm Patricia LaVoice," I said as I reached for her hand. It was small in mine, but her handshake was firm.

"Hello, I'm so happy to finally get to meet you. I am Terese Payne."

We sat and spoke most of the evening. She told me where to go in San Francisco to shop and dine, and what doctors and dentist to use for the kids. She gave me directions to the Catholic church in town and recommended a private school for Olivia. She spoke about her teenaged daughter, getting her ready for college, and what it was like raising a child while having a career. I learned she had been diagnosed with lupus, a chronic autoimmune disease, a year earlier, and that her doctors had insisted she retire immediately. I asked her what it had been like, working in a man's world.

"When I started my career in the investment business there were no women in sales, only clerical positions. It was a man's game—their field, their ball, their bat. I had to learn to play by their rules and work twice as hard to hit the home runs."

Her expression became very serious, and then she smiled. "You know, when I first started out, my manager wouldn't even let me sit for the Series 7, but I got around him and scored higher than anyone else."

"Was it hard working with so many men?"

"Funny, all my mentors were men. I enjoyed being a woman in a man's world. I saw it as an advantage, certainly, with my institutional clients. I wouldn't have become the first female partner nor the first female regional partner without their advice, encouragement, and sometimes, total disbelief. My CEO and mentor once said to a group of partners he was trying to motivate, "You know that girl on the West Coast? Follow her. You might get it right!"

I was completely intrigued by Terese Payne. She was nothing at all like the image I had painted of her, based on secondhand stories. In reality, she had the determination and power of an Eleanor Roosevelt. She was a true lady who was probably more successful than any other person in the room. Those General Patton stories now seemed the result of envy.

I worked my parents' death into the conversation. I always managed to squeeze my story in. No matter who I was talking to, or where I was, I got my story told. After three years, I was still hoping someone would say something to help me make sense of my loss, or relieve some of my pain.

"I'm sorry," she said, and I waited for the usual uncomfortable silence, but she didn't even flinch. Instead, she reached for my hand. Instinctively, I pulled back, but stopped myself and let her. "I lost my mother when I was young, and I understand how painful life can be."

I had heard a million words of consolation by then. I'd kept myself hidden in pregnancies and nursing, creating and nurturing others. I talked about the accident all the time, but acted as if it had happened to someone else. It was a way to shield myself. This time my defense mechanism failed me. I could not conjure up any mental windows to shatter to distract myself, and the tears started to flow. It was too painful for me to look into her familiar-seeming eyes, and I excused myself from the table. It was not the time nor the place for me to mourn. As I walked away, I was haunted by her striking resemblance to my mother.

🌳 🌳 🌳

I WORKED FOR TERESE'S FRIENDSHIP like I would work a high school crush. She was very busy. Her days were full of doctor's appointments, calls to insurance companies, and getting her daughter started in college. She was always gracious to hear from me, but she didn't have the time, interest, or energy for a new friendship. I understood and respected that, so I cherished every phone call. We spoke about my children's education and her travels to Europe and other interesting places.

We kept our conversations light, our boundaries set, something I was desperately trying to learn to do. It was not my nature to monitor my speech, but it was a much-needed skill for my new role. Rich's business often required entertaining clients. In the beginning, Rich would poke at me under the table to let me know if I had crossed the boundary of acceptable conversation. He stopped doing that when I started saying, "Honey, did you just poke me?" Now I was doing my best to reform myself.

After a decent interval of time had passed, and our phone conversations had progressed, I invited Terese to the house for some tea. I opened the door with a baby on my boob, a toddler at my hip, holding a bologna sandwich in my hand. The bologna dropped to the floor, and I quickly picked it up, gave it a swipe on my pant leg, and folded it back into the bread before handing it to Billy. Olivia could be heard laughing in the background.

"Hi! Come in," I said.

Terese immediately reached for Billy, who went to her without hesitation. Olivia came flying down the stairs on a bright red sled and jumped up, as if the world belonged to her.

"Hi, I'm Olivia. Do you want to see my room?"

Terese looked at me in total amazement. "What is she doing?"

"I'm sledding!" Olivia exclaimed, surprised that it was not obvious.

"I was raised back East," I explained. "I hate that my kids miss out on winter sports, so we sled down the stairs."

"Isn't that dangerous?"

"Probably."

Her expression was priceless. My children were always dirty and usually half-dressed, if dressed at all, but they were happy. I never used a playpen and barely a crib. I wanted them to feel free and know that they were always my center. I offered Terese a chair, and Olivia climbed onto her lap.

"You smell pretty," Olivia stated as she buried her face in Terese's chest.

"Olivia, give her space," I said.

"She's fine," Terese replied.

The two of them were immediately lost in conversation about fairies, princesses, and magical castles. Terese mesmerized all the children with her extraordinary imagination and storytelling abilities. Billy was hanging on every word. There was so much love in the room, a spell she created. She made each child feel special, a priceless gift. Just the day before at the neighborhood park, I'd heard a woman complaining, "Whenever my mother comes over, she wakes the baby up from her nap to kiss her. Can't she wait?"

"Who cares?" I'd whispered. "Rock the baby back to sleep, you ungrateful fool. I would give anything to have my mother wake up one of my babies with too many kisses."

Thoughts like these had become a part of my inner battle. I listened to the world around me focus on insignificant matters, putting so much energy into the negative. *Don't they get it?* I'd fume. *This is not a dress rehearsal, and it can all be gone in the morning!*

An hour after she arrived, Terese hugged and kissed the children goodbye. As I walked her to the front door, she casually mentioned that Robert, her husband, was out of town and that she had to go to the hospital for a chemotherapy treatment in the morning.

"Lupus causes the immune system to attack the body's own tissue and organs," she explained. "The immune system normally protects the body, but with lupus, the body loses the ability to tell the difference between foreign substances and its own cells and tissue."

"In other words, your body is creating a war within itself?"

With a sad smile, she nodded. "The doctors are hoping the chemo will kill the bad cells that are attacking my organs."

"May I go with you?" I asked. "Rich will be home, so he can watch the children."

After a pause she said, "I would love your company."

CHAPTER 5

Looking at Life While Facing the End

My mother is so angry at me. Why is she so angry? She never gets angry at me.

"Talk to me! Why are you so mad? What did I do?" She turns her back and I'm shocked. Never in my life can I remember her being so mad at me. Once in eighth grade we got in a big fight and I was mean, but I had not said a hurtful thing to her since, and I could not remember one hurtful thing she had ever said to me.

"Mother, what is wrong? Am I dreaming?"

I forced myself to wake up. I was so confused. What did it mean? Why would she come to me in a dream and be mad? Had I done something wrong? Did I say something she did not like? Is she mad I cursed at God?

No, she would not be mad that I cursed at God. I bet she was pretty mad at Him too. I know I would be if my children were hurting so badly and that was years ago. My mother never gets mad at me.

That morning it was cold and foggy as I drove nervously over the Golden Gate Bridge to meet Terese. Something about not having the option to pull over or stop left me feeling panicked when I drove across bridges—something that never bothered me before my parents' accident. I approached the traffic light at Marine Street and slammed on the brakes as the light turned from yellow to red. I had also learned to hate traffic lights. My body tensed as I watched in my rearview mirror for the car behind me to come to a complete stop.

How different would life be today if my father had not stopped that night? Sometimes I wondered: What if he had made it through the traffic light? Was it yellow when he stopped? I never learned how long the light had been red before they were hit. And now, at every red light, I have to trust the stranger behind me. They have my life in their hands. I sat waiting at the light thinking, *Bam*. The second it turned from red to green, I was gone, moving, safe.

I pulled into the hospital parking lot and walked down the endless halls looking for the chemotherapy section. I hung my head low, offering privacy to the other patients, although I was shamefully curious of why they were there. Each room I passed had a story to tell. While the world outside was going on without missing a beat, people driving to work, getting their morning coffee, kissing their children goodbye, there was nothing ordinary about the day for the families within these walls.

When I reached Terese's room, I paused and took a deep breath, and my heart sank. There she lay, half-awake, defenseless in blue-and-white-checkered hospital threads. Her eyes did not seem as blue this morning, and her cheeks sank deeper into her face than I remembered.

"Tricia! I'm so glad you made it before they inserted the needle."

"Hey, I wouldn't miss that for anything," I joked.

"I have a real issue with needles," said Terese. "One too many bad experiences as a child."

A young nurse with a flawless complexion came in to hang a clear bag of fluid on the IV tree. "It should take about three hours for the contents of the bag to empty."

Empty, I thought. It sounded so simple. The bag just had to empty, deplete itself. Chemicals in that little bag could save her life, but they'd also destroy healthy cells. Like all wars, destruction would be left behind. Terese was praying the chemo would win, but she knew she would pay a heavy price.

I walked to the window and looked out to the world. Two hospital attendees sat on a wall talking. A woman walked by with her dog.

"Do you want me to close the shades?" I asked. "It's bright in here."

"Just lower them so we get some morning sun."

I struggled with the cord, steering sunlight though the window, then sat carefully on the edge of the bed. The thought of reaching for her hand entered my mind, but I resisted. When the nurse approached, Terese held out her arm, tightening the muscles in her face and biting down on her lower lips. The room was silent and still as if life had stopped for a moment. I placed my hand on top of hers, feeling her bones. Without hesitation, she folded her hand around mine. As her grip grew tighter, I was surprised to find that I was the one who felt comforted.

As the nurse inserted the needle, Terese lay back, closing her eyes. I assumed she was praying. An orderly brought in some extra pillows and a blanket to make her comfortable. Now, all we had to do was wait.

"I had no idea how serious lupus is," I confessed.

"Most people don't. It's primarily a women's disease. Many people think it's psychological." She gestured to the chemo drip. "Does this look psychological to you?"

I felt ashamed to be one of those people. "I'm so sorry, Terese."

"We need to raise money for research and education. We need to find a cure."

We stayed there for three hours, me at the foot of the bed, Terese sitting upright with the IV connected to her arm.

My favorite thing to do with my mother was to lie on her bed and talk with her about absolutely everything and absolutely nothing. I did it my whole life, but the time we spent together on her bed right before the accident became priceless, because I had a nursing baby at my breast. We were three generations of women talking comfortably on the bed. How utterly perfect were those moments?

She asked quietly, "Do you pray?"

Immediately, my eyes went to the window. *Smash!* My mind drove my foot straight through the glass pane.

"I stopped praying when my parents died. Before...I used to pray for a deeper faith. I remember being thirteen and wishing my faith was deeper. I thought when my parents died my faith would finally become stronger. But instead I just stopped praying altogether."

"Do you ever talk to your parents?" she asked.

"Oh, God no! That would make it unbearably real, that they are really gone and never coming back. This way I can pretend they are away on a long vacation or something."

I smashed another window and then another.

"Were you in San Francisco during the big earthquake?" I asked.

"Tricia, don't change the subject."

"I'm not," I insisted. "I was here, and I remember thinking we were going to die. I was absolutely terrified. Seeing the fires and hearing the public service announcements over the radio. It was horrific. Two days after the earthquake, I went to UCSF hospital to volunteer in the pediatric unit, doing puppet therapy for the children going in for operations and the kids getting chemotherapy. There was one unit no one was allowed in unless you covered yourself with hospital scrubs and washed your hands and arms in this special orange soap for ten minutes—literally ten minutes. It was always silent and a little eerie, because you knew the kids in this unit were really sick. There was a little girl, around six years old, bright yellow hair, sweet face. An older woman—her grandmother, I suppose—was sitting with her. I asked about the earthquake, because that was all anyone was talking about. Where were you? Were you scared? Did you get hurt? The grandmother was bewildered. She just looked at me with a blank face and said, 'What earthquake?'"

Terese played with the edge of her blanket, crunching the silky edge into a ball in the palm of her hand. "Do you talk to God?"

"You do not want to know the last thing I said to God." I busted my whole fist through the remaining windowpane. "Haven't talked to him since right after the accident, not even when Billy was in the ICU as an infant. What good would praying do? Look where it got me the night my parents were killed. I prayed, bargained, pleaded, said I would take even one of them, even all broken up. I'd care for them forever. But no. So yeah..." *Fuck him*, I thought with satisfaction.

Terese remained silent.

"I'm confused about God," I admitted. "Everyone talks about how much he loves us and how he sacrificed his son for us, and for that I give him credit. But what about the millions of people who lose whole families? When you send your son or daughter off to war, aren't you risking a sacrifice? When God's son died he went to be with God—no one else gets that?"

I wanted a good answer. I wanted to love God again and understand. I really wanted it all to mean something, to believe that there was a reason for my parents' death besides some asshole speeding through a red light. Speak, Terese. Say something powerful. Make sense of my loss. Help me.

She took my hand and suggested, "Maybe you could try talking to God again. I understand you're angry, but maybe you could just try."

There was an uncomfortable silence. I wasn't going to lie: I was not ready for forgiveness or acceptance.

"Tell me about your mother," I said.

"I had one older sister who was ten, a brother who was eight, me, my brother who was two and three months, and my brother who was ten months. She was pregnant with my youngest brother, born almost three months premature, just a couple of hours before she died. He lived. My father had suffered so much during the war, his capture by Rommel in North Africa, where he had been sent by Patton to deploy the mobile bridges they had engineered. The march from the boot of Italy over the Alps to Poland by the SS, his escape, the six months to make it to England. The long trip home. The only constants, his faith and his love for his childhood friend, his sweetheart, his wife. Six months after she died, he was sent to the Korean War. He believed General MacArthur was right in his fight against the communists. It was his duty. He left us with my mother's only sister not quite seven months after my mother's death. A year later, the state removed us from our home and her care. We were sent to the local orphanage, whose inhabitants were children with mental, emotional, and physical problems more often than having no parents. When my sister and brother went missing from school, the nuns from St. Benedict's started searching. Once found, they came each morning and picked the three of us up. Not old enough to go to school, I stayed with them at the motherhouse, my very own private school. They returned us each afternoon. They were a blessing from Mary."

How grossly unfair. She just had life growing inside of her. She had five young children who needed her, and she still died. Yet, Terese wanted me to forgive God. We left the hospital quietly, much closer to each other—and I felt much more exposed, knowing I was going home to a husband I adored and three young children full of love and life, while faithful Terese would go home to suffer physical hell as the side effects of the chemotherapy set in.

🌱 🌱 🌱

AT ABOUT 3:30 A.M., Billy cried out, frightened by a bad dream.

"Mommy! Mommy!"

I jumped up and ran down the dark hallway. I held him tight, rocking him gently. I smelled his hair and rubbed his back and was so grateful that I could restore peace to his little world. Billy was not much younger than Terese when her mother died. I pictured her at four years old in her little pink nightgown, half-awake with eyes wet from tears as she cried out for the love and comfort of a mother who could not come. I ached to hold her close to me and make it all better. I ached to take her little hand in mine and tell her everything was going to be all right.

I loved spoiling my mother with flowers and pictures, or anything that reminded her of how much I loved her, so I bought Terese flowers the following day. As I passed through the ivy-covered entrance gate and meandered up the long, steep driveway, I felt as if I had entered a secret door to France. Terese had created her own French château on the top of the hill with black iron gates and romantic balconies. The serene English gardens were accented with life-sized statues and water fountains. Inside, Terese had created a winding stairway with walls painted like old stone, emulating the Petit Trianon at Versailles. The windows stretched from floor to ceiling, showcasing views of the valley below. Terese had a room shipped from France from a château being stripped, not far from Josephine's Château de Malmaison. What was once a king's waiting room was now a stunning library. Every room in the house was straight out of *Architectural Digest*.

I found Terese in the green, in the shade of her Japanese maples, sun protection clothing covering her limbs. She wore a floppy straw hat to protect her face. Sun and heat have very negative effects on people with lupus; it activates the disease, making them physically ill with acute joint pain and pounding headaches.

I was relieved to see she had rebounded from the chemotherapy, although I suspected she hid her pain well. We walked as she told me the history behind the Greek statues and pointed out the flowers she was proudest of growing. The faint sounds of insects could be heard over the melody of birds chirping. It felt as if time stood still and nothing could harm us there. We talked about how Rich was doing at the office, and she asked me how the children were.

"Crazy good," I said. "Olivia asked the other day if you had visited while she and the others were out. When I said you hadn't, she commented that she thought you had, because she could smell you in the house. That's a good thing."

Terese's strong commitment to the church, the fact that she surrounded herself with beauty, and her ability to enjoy each moment, all seemed more understandable. She had become a warrior at the age of four, but she'd won the battle. She did not indulge in self-pity, nor did she abuse herself or self-destruct. She chose life and grew more loving.

Now I sat with her, embracing that love, and also choosing life.

※ ※ ※

I SAW LITTLE OF TERESE between her treatments. I would meet her at Sunday Mass with Rich and the kids, but otherwise, I stayed away. She was so susceptible to catching germs, and God knows, the kids and I had germs. I began to worry about the germs she exposed herself to at church after I read about the large amount of germs found in the holy water. She would not consider entering the church without reaching for a blessing, so I would bring antibacterial hand wipes in my purse and encourage her to wipe down after she dipped.

I was envious of her strong faith. She would take every precaution to stay healthy, but inside the church walls, she would shake hands and hug half the people in our town. I would stand over her shoulder paying close attention to everyone she touched. It was vital that she stay healthy during her treatments. Chemotherapy broke down her immune system. Interestingly, she never caught anything from her exchanges of peace and love on those Sunday mornings. As weak as her immune system had become, the need for the human heart to be nurtured must have been greater.

I felt the warmth and love between parishioners on those Sunday mornings. I'd recite the prayers I learned in my childhood and bless those I loved. I listened to the homily carefully, and let the music touch my soul. But I didn't apologize to God for saying, "Fuck you." I was still mad and not ready to ask for forgiveness. I hoped God was willing to give me time.

On the morning of Terese's next chemotherapy session, rain poured down harder than I had ever seen in San Francisco. The Golden Gate Bridge was completely fogged in, and the city's skyline was invisible. Again, I stopped at the light at Marine Street. There was no one behind me. Suddenly, I saw a car approaching, coming up on me quickly. Or maybe he wasn't. My heart pounded in my chest. I looked helplessly to the car stopped in the lane next to me. A young woman spoke on her cell phone, twirling her gum. The car behind me got closer. I thought of going through the traffic light, but feared getting hit by cross traffic. He got closer. Closer. He stopped. He stopped, and I was safe, but I could hardly breathe.

After checking in with Terese, I went to the cafeteria and got us both some tea. I hated why we were there and would have done anything to change it, but I loved sitting at the foot of her bed. We'd talk, giving each other undivided attention.

"How is the praying going?" she asked me.

"When you and I are at church, I say the Our Father and I thank God for my life," I admitted. "And I say blessings for the people I love."

"Very safe."

"Very. I just don't want to go there right now," I replied. "The other day Rich had to fly to New York. Normally I would pray for him to have a safe trip, but everyone is telling me 'things happen for a reason' and 'God has a plan.' So what good does praying do for his safety? If his time is up, it doesn't matter how much I pray."

"You have to talk about your mom and dad, about the accident, Tricia. You can't keep it all bottled up inside of you."

"I'd rather pretend they're on a trip to some incredible paradise."

"They are." She smiled.

I shot her a disapproving look.

I wasn't buying the cliché: they are in a happier place now, and you will be with them soon. I wanted to go to lunch with them now! I wanted to show them my children's artwork and tell them about how successful Rich was and how happy we were. People say, "Don't worry, Tricia, they know." Well, I wanted to tell them myself, on Christmas morning, on birthdays, on ordinary days. I did not want to hear platitudes from anyone who could pick up the phone and call their mother and father. If you can call yours, then don't tell me that mine are "with me in spirit," goddammit!

I ached so desperately to have them with me. I would fantasize about what it would be like if I found out the accident had all been an act and they'd needed to disappear for a while. I would pretend they were secret agents and the government had faked their death for all our safety. I imagined what their homecoming would be like and how much I had to tell them. I tried to make a deal with God to give them back to me for just two hours, and I would spend every day of my life working for the good of other people. I would tell God to take my right arm, take ten years of my life, if only he would give me two hours. Just two hours. How could it be possible that I would never again say, "Hi, Mom, how was your day? What's Dad doing? Have you thought about what flowers you're planting this spring?"

"I do talk about the accident," I said. "I think a major thing people who have not experienced loss don't get is how much time is needed. They think you should be getting over it because a few years have passed. Shit, that's just the beginning. For me, the first couple years after the accident are a blur. I was holding my breath waiting to scream. My brain had to adjust to the thought that I no longer had a mother or father. I had to go over it again, and again, and again, and I had to rethink the actual moment of their deaths over and over again, the impact of their car being hit. Every traffic light I stop at, I wait for someone to slam into the back of me. This is my normal." I elbowed her gently. "There, I talked about it. Happy?"

"It's a start." Terese smiled, triumphant.

"Do you think I will always be the girl whose parents died in the car accident? When people describe me to their friends, is that how they will define me?"

"It happened five years ago in Pennsylvania," she replied. "Why does everyone you've met in Mill Valley know about it?"

"Because that is who I am: a wife, a mother, and the girl whose parents died in an accident. It's a part of me, and I don't know how to separate it from the rest of my life. Just like I tell everyone that I'm married with children, I tell them about my parents."

"If that is who you think you are, then that is how people will see you. Is that how you want to be seen?"

"I would have to say, yes. Right now in my life, I do not think I can be anyone but that girl whose parents died."

"Then that is who you will be for right now."

The other night Olivia flipped out, crying so hard she could barely catch her breath, saying she missed her grandma and it wasn't fair because she would never get to see her again. She was mourning. And I realized that every time her understanding matures another notch, she'll have to mourn all over again. Of course, we tell them all the wonderful things about my parents, but it's impossible to keep their memory alive and not make the kids sad. It's like telling them about chocolate ice cream, how good it tastes, and then saying, 'Oh, by the way, you'll never taste it. Your friends have ice cream, but yours is all gone.'"

"What did you say to Olivia?"

"I told her I missed them too and then took her into the backyard to swing on the swings. It was dark out, so she got a kick out of that."

Terese remained silent.

"I asked a friend of mine—a therapist—if she thought Olivia needed to talk to someone."

"What did she say?"

"She said I'm the one who needs the therapist and Olivia is picking up on my grief."

"Do you agree with her?" she asked.

"Probably, but I have three babies—hopefully a fourth soon. There's no way I could go into therapy right now and dig up ugly thoughts. I have to distance myself from the pain and raise my children."

"Okay, but you understand that eventually you'll need to work through it, don't you?"

"I did see a wonderful therapist in New York right after they were killed. My mind was so utterly fried and my heart so broken.

She helped me find the strength to function as a mother and wife. Olivia and Rich needed me, so dying was not an option."

"So the therapist helped?" Terese pushed.

"I suppose. At our last session, she said she thought our work together was good, but we never really touched on my mother's death. I was stunned by that. I thought I had talked about my mother the whole time. She was my soul mate, my best friend, my strength. She knew me better than I knew myself."

Terese looked sad. She had never experienced what I now mourned.

"Do you still miss your mom?" I asked.

"I don't think a girl ever stops missing her mother."

"Do you remember the night she died?"

"I remember the night I said goodbye to her. They wheeled her out to us. We were all standing in the hall—my father, my older brother and sister, and me. It was late. My younger brothers, both babies, were left at home sleeping. I remember so clearly how beautiful she was. She was wearing a pink nightgown. I climbed up on her lap and played with her long, black, beautiful hair. Snuggling as close as I could get. She held me and kissed me and held my brother's and sister's hands to her face until Daddy said to give Mommy a kiss. I never questioned everyone's tears. She held me close, whispered, 'I love you.'

"I never saw her again.

"The phone rang that night shortly after 1 a.m. It was the hospital. It woke me; I could hear whispering and crying. I went downstairs where everyone was huddled on my parents' bed, crying in each other's arms, softly, so as not to wake the baby in the crib at the end of the bed. I never saw her again. The world I knew was forever changed that night. I didn't understand. I kept asking for her. Nobody told me anything. They didn't take me to the funeral. I have often wondered over the years, why not?

"Before my father left for Korea, he took us to see 'Mommy.' It was a pretty place, lots of grass and big stones on a knoll. Just above and beyond the big tree was a scene from Calvary. I never forgot that. I couldn't understand how Mommy could be there, where?"

It struck me that Terese had spent only four years with her mother, and the rest of her life she'd spent missing her.

"You want to hear a funny story about my therapist?" I asked.

"Sure," said Terese.

"In her waiting room and office, I noticed all the pictures on the walls were women with sad expressions on their faces. Inside her office, more pictures of women with sad faces. I made a number of snarky comments about how depressing they were, and she listened but didn't say anything. Over a year later, I spotted a picture of clowns dancing right behind her head. I asked her, 'When did you hang that picture?' And she said, 'It's been there ever since you've been coming to therapy.' That's how good a therapist she was! She recognized I was in no place to see dancing clowns. She accepted my sniping about her decor and never pointed out the clowns to me. She waited until I was ready to see them for myself."

Terese smiled. "Tricia, it's going to be okay. You'll be all right."

My eyes quickly filled, and I nodded. How well she understood my pain. This was just four years after the death of my parents, and most people close to me would say I was doing great. I spoke to my closest girlfriends regularly, the girls I'd grown up with, who knew and loved my parents, and they thought I was fine. Terese was able to see how much pain I was still in, probably because she was the only person I let in.

She understood that time had taken away the rawness of the pain, but the loss lingered.

"I hope we have twenty years before Olivia gets married. Will you be at her wedding?" My heart began to pound. I knew she would be honest, and we never spoke of her life expectancy.

Terese looked at me with my mother's soft blue eyes. "Yes."

I felt so relieved, but deep down we both knew nothing was certain. Some days she felt good, but most of the time she felt extreme fatigue and ached all over. The swelling in her hands, and the low-grade fever she continuously ran were constant reminders that she was not well. We weren't related; she had no obligations to my family or me, but she chose to love us like her own. I could not bear to lose her.

CHAPTER 6

Closer to Tears of Joy and Sorrow

Everything Terese touched felt so special, unique. She was gifted at creating beauty in the world. She focused on the small things and made every moment count. Whenever I went to Terese's home, my children would plead, "Please, Mommy, please, can we go?"

"Just promise not to touch anything," would be my last words as we got out of the car, and "Don't touch! Don't touch!" would be my only words the whole time we were there. Olivia always escaped to the downstairs bedroom, which hosted a magnificent dollhouse replica of Tara from *Gone with the Wind*. Terese had all the characters made and costumed exactly from the movie. Billy and Jack just loved running around the gardens, fascinated by the statues and hiding places.

I loved introducing Terese to my high school friends when they visited.

"I lost my breath," Amy told me. "She looks so much like your mother."

❦ ❦ ❦

I WAS HOT ON THE TRAIL of baby number four at the time and, once again, I encountered that faint blue line on a home pregnancy test. Thrilled, I couldn't wait to tell Terese the news. But I started to bleed the next day. She listened to me cry over the phone and said, "Oh, honey, my arms are around you." And I swear, I felt her arms around me. For the first time, I wondered if my mother had sent her.

Olivia turned six, Billy turned four, and Jack turned two. Summer was coming to an end. September was upon us—the month I'd come to dread—bringing the fifth anniversary of my parents' deaths. It was an odd milestone marked by a certain expectation of healing. Life had gone on. Babies had been born, friends married, jobs changed, and my parents weren't there for any of it.

Somewhere around 7:15 p.m. Eastern Standard Time on September 16, 1993, an impact had taken place. Every minute between 7:15 to 8:30 hurt; I knew that during this time my parents were spectacles for rubberneckers, their bodies cold and exposed.

On the day of the anniversary, Terese told me, "Be ready at four o'clock. Bring a sweater and a towel."

I had no idea what she had planned, but Rich came home early to watch the children. Terese and I drove into the city for a massage and an early movie. As I watched the love story unfold, I realized that it was 7:45 p.m. I had missed the moment of impact that haunted me. I leaned over to Terese and showed her my watch. She smiled and touched my hand.

After the movie, we went across the street for dinner and sat talking until they closed the restaurant. Terese told me the long, twisted story of how she ended up living with her alcoholic aunt while her father was away fighting for his country. Her aunt used to send her to the store—a five-year-old!—to buy wine in a brown jug. By the time she was seven, she was the primary caretaker of her little brothers.

"I'd line them up in a row on the floor and change their diapers," she said. "I remember being cold all the time. I'd go down into the basement and lift this huge iron bar up, so that I could shovel the coal into a furnace that took up the whole room. The shovel was very heavy. It was easier to try to throw the larger pieces in, but I was afraid of the fire. Tired, I would sit in the corner savoring the warmth until I had to go up."

"What do you think your mom thought was going to happen to her babies once she was gone?" I asked.

"Years ago, I found a deed for a farmhouse signed months before she died. We were Army brats and lived on base, so there was no reason for her to have bought that land except for her children. She would have been devastated to know how it all played out. She was a smart woman, earned her B.A. back when very few women attended college. I'm sure she thought through a plan for her family before she died."

"So she died thinking her husband would raise her six babies on a beautiful farm in Virginia, and instead her drunken sister raised them in poverty?"

"I wish I could ask my father what he was thinking," said Terese. "Why would he leave us like that? During those last months, did they talk about what would come next? Did he assure her of the plan?"

"How did you get away from your aunt?" I asked as we crossed the quiet street to Terese's black Mercedes Coupe.

"One night she got incredibly drunk and began to beat my older brother with a baseball bat until he no longer moved. I was terrified. I knew where the phone was; I lifted the receiver and told the operator my brother was dead. My aunt was beating him with a baseball bat. She was drinking. She didn't really notice me carry, one by one, my three little brothers upstairs to the front bedroom, my sister's bedroom. The windows opened onto the front porch roof. That's how she escaped out of the house every night. I locked the door. Soon I heard my aunt yelling, 'Open the door!'

"I sat huddled on the bed holding my three little brothers. She stopped screaming. It was very quiet. I thought she had fallen asleep like she always did, eventually. The first thud of the hammer on the door stopped my heart, Tricia. I moved each one of the babies to the floor next to the window. She just kept screaming and hammering. She had broken through one piece. I could see her flushed face, then the police were everywhere. That's all I remember. Later, I realized we now lived in this great big place with separate buildings. I was in the big house. We were all separated; girls twelve and up, boys eight to ten and up, the smaller ones separated by gender. Once I was brought to see my three little brothers, as they had smallpox and were in this glass box. I cried and cried. My sister was always running away. She would come to the fence that separated our buildings and tell me goodbye and warn me not to say anything. They always brought her back. I believe I created a fantasy world from the Sunday comics. My bed was by a window; my best friend never spoke. We had to have a teaspoon of apricot nectar every night before bed. I hated Friday-night dinners. It was liver. I had made my First Holy Communion before my father left for Korea. I knew I couldn't eat meat on Friday. They would make me sit at that long refractory table until midnight every Friday night for five years. I never ate the liver. But then at Christmas, we always got to choose whatever we wanted from this big box of clothes. No one was mean to me that I remember. A couple desperately wanted to adopt me. I liked them a lot. They came on Sundays and would push me on the swing. They stopped coming. My father said no. That's it mostly."

"You must have been an adorable little girl," I commented.

"Who knows?" she said with a soft smile and sparkling eyes. "I never saw a picture of myself as a child."

"What do you mean, you never saw a picture of yourself?"

"Who would be taking pictures of me?" she said. "When my sister left home, she took most of my mother's belongings, including the few photos that existed."

I sat in the passenger seat, pondering all this. Terese's birthday was approaching, and I had been thinking long and hard about something special to give her. How I could get a hold of those photographs of Terese as a young girl? It would be way out of line for me to try to contact her sister, since they hadn't spoken in decades, but I'd met Terese's sister-in-law once when she was visiting Terese. I thought she might be able to help me. And in fact, she did a few months later. It gave me such joy to send those photos to Terese, who was overwhelmed when she received them.

We drove in silence toward the Golden Gate Bridge, stopping at the traffic signal on Lombard and Green. When the light turned green, I blurted, "*Go!*"

Terese tried not to appear startled.

"Sorry," I said, embarrassed.

"For what?" She shrugged.

We crossed the Golden Gate Bridge and cruised through the former Army base above the San Francisco Bay. We passed abandoned barracks and a working habitat for nature. It was after eleven, and the place was deserted. The only light was from the stars and the moon above and the beautiful skyline of San Francisco. Terese pulled over and parked the car.

"Come on," she said. "Let's go down to the beach."

I followed her across the sand, and we laid out a towel to sit on. Terese had a Bible tucked under her arm. She lit a candle and began to read.

I remember feeling at that moment that I wanted to be sad. I felt like she expected me to be sad, and if I cried, she would feel better about her efforts. She wanted me to let some of the pain out, but at that moment, my walls were up, and they were not coming down. She read from the Bible for about ten minutes; I don't remember the words or the passage. Then she reached inside her bag and brought out ten gardenias, eight white and two yellow.

"Each white flower represents a year since their death," she said, "and the yellow represent this year, for remembrance, happiness, and joy."

We walked down to the ocean and rolled up our pants legs. The sea sloshed up my leg and soaked my jeans. Terese handed me the flowers and, one by one, I tossed them into the ocean, first the white and then the yellow. I did not cry. But I didn't hurt either. At that moment, I simply took refuge in Terese's love.

The house was dark when I returned, so I quietly entered and found my way through the dark to kiss and smell the children as they slept. I climbed in bed and nestled up to Rich. He stirred and asked how

I was doing. I replied I was good, and he kissed my forehead before drifting back to sleep. I did not hurt. I felt only love and gratitude.

That night, I said a quick prayer:

Dear God, thank you for all the wonderful things in my life. Thank you for my beautiful children and for Rich and my sisters and all my wonderful friends. Thank you for Terese's love. Please watch after them all. God, I am sorry I cursed at you. I did not mean it. I'm just very confused about a lot of things in my life. I love you. Goodnight.

🌿 🌿 🌿

"YOU NEVER TALK about the man who killed your parents," Terese said as we sat her dining room table having tea.

"No, he's not deserving of my time. I would have forgiven him if he contacted us and said he was sorry for our loss. But he never did, so fuck him."

"Maybe he didn't know how to contact you?"

"He could have found us if he wanted to. He sideswiped another car before plowing into the back of my parents' car. A witness at the scene said after he hit the first car, he took full control of his car, moved back into my parents' lane and then accelerated. He said he had a seizure. Obviously, the judge did not believe him. He was sent to prison."

"How long did he serve?"

I paused before answering and stared at the window in front of me. I kicked and I kicked and I kicked. "The maximum sentence in Pennsylvania for vehicular manslaughter is two years, which he received, but he probably served one and then probation." Glass flew everywhere. "There were no drugs or alcohol involved. He had just gone through a fast-food drive-through. He was probably speeding down the road while looking for a French fry. Did he mean to kill anyone that night? No, but his irresponsible actions took my parents' lives. He should have admitted that and apologized."

"He didn't speak in court?" Terese asked.

"He did, but it was only to tell us how depressed he had become. In other words, how the accident had affected his life. Maybe he said he was sorry, but I disregard anything he said that day. He was standing in front of a judge who was about to sentence him to jail. His words meant nothing to me. He had seven months before the court day to contact us. And he's had many years since. Never a word."

I looked to her and could not handle her uncanny resemblance to my mother. I reached back and took the hair tie from my hair. "Terese, could you please pull your hair back?"

She did not even question this out-of-place request. She took the tie from my hand and pulled the hair from her face.

"I know if I was responsible for killing two people that I would make every effort to ask forgiveness from their family," I continued.

Terese sat quietly and let me vent.

"We never even sued, because we heard he was a single parent and we did not want to hurt the child. I can't remember his face or what he looked like. I know he is white, around thirty, and I think his hair is brown. I never saw him again, only that one time in court."

I got up from the table and walked over to the window.

I turned back to Terese. Her eyes met mine and I admitted, "He not only took my parents from me. For a time, he took my ability to parent."

I took a deep breath. "A few months after the accident, I had a terrifying dream about the accident. I woke up so disoriented and miserable. I remember sitting on the couch just staring off into space. Olivia was playing around me humming nursery rhymes. She was naked and barefoot. There was a picture on the floor that I was in the middle of framing. I had twice asked her to stay away from it, but she was two and had a mind of her own. She walked on top of the glass, and I smacked her butt hard and she cried a lot. Her tiny white behind had my big ugly red handprint on it. I didn't dress her. I kept her naked, so I would have to stare at what I had done. I hated myself. My parents would have been irate at the thought of me laying a hand on my child. If the accident had never happened, I would have had more patience for her, I would have been happier for her, I would have been a better mother to her when she was little. I hate him for that too." I put my head down in shame.

"So you do hate him?"

"I know hating him hurts me. But I'm not ready to forgive him. Maybe I never will be."

However, I did wonder how the accident had changed his life. Had he grown from it, and if so, what had he learned? I wondered how horrible it must be to lie in bed at night and, just before you drift off to sleep, realize your recklessness took the lives of two people. Did he not need our understanding and forgiveness to achieve peace? I would have given it to him if he had asked. I am sure of that.

I wonder, does he wake up and say, "Today is a good day. I am happy to be alive." I'm curious, in some perverse way, if it felt empowering to have ended life? I know how empowering it felt to begin life. We give God credit for starting life. Did he think God had a part in aiding him in ending their lives? That my parents' time was up and God used him as the tool to take them out?

I'm shocked that he never wanted to contact us, and cry with us. My parents were now an intimate part of his life. How could he not want to know everything about them? He should have had the decency to talk to us and tell us how sorry he was for what happened. That is what you do: you say you are sorry when you hurt someone, even if you did not mean to hurt them.

🌱 🌱 🌱

RICH AND I HAD PLANNED on having two kids spaced three years apart. We would travel and I would earn my doctorate. After the accident, my plans changed. If two people were prematurely taken from me, I would create two more people. After Jack was born, Rich put the brakes on. He felt that three were all we could handle. I understood his point; however, I created this fourth child in my mind and was determined to have her.

Everyone around me was growing sick of hearing about my desire to have a fourth. I'd talked to everyone and anyone about it. I'd told Terese, I'd told my sisters, I'd told my girlfriends, the mailman, and anyone sitting next to me at a dinner.

Rich and I had some serious discussions and fights about the matter.

When at social events—or even sitting in the park—I would talk to women no longer in their childbearing years who said they wanted another child, but their husbands did not. They said the void never goes away. I knew that at the end of my life I could regret not traveling enough or not earning a doctorate, but I never wanted to regret not having a child I was meant to have. I realized that I was putting our marriage in jeopardy, but I felt that strongly about it. I don't think I would have pushed so hard if my parents were alive, but my need to procreate was overwhelming. Some nights I would stand in the hallway when everyone was sleeping. The house would be still and peaceful. I would close my eyes and feel the love from my children, but I also could feel someone missing. I would go into each of the children's rooms and look at their precious faces as they dreamed, while feeling deep inside me that someone was not home. I do not know what I said that finally pushed Rich over to my side probably the threat of marriage counseling. Or maybe it was the fact that life was going well for us, so he caved. I jumped, literally, on the opportunity, and before he could change his mind I dialed our sex life back up to what it had been in our honeymoon days. I pulled out my best lingerie and made sure I was in bed every night when he was. I became every married man's dream wife.

One month later, we sat down at the dinner table and Olivia opened with, "Dylan Brugger and Carl Wright want to come over tomorrow and shoot Daddy's gun."

"What?" Rich is not a gun person and has never owned one.

"I heard Mommy on the phone last night tell her friend that you shot a loaded gun."

If looks could kill, I would be dead.

🌱 🌱 🌱

AT WEEK TWENTY, when Rich and I went in for my sonogram, I was certain I was carrying a daughter. I could picture the news being delivered. Olivia came along—and she wanted a sister so badly. The technician entered the room, and I took my position on the bed. She coated my bare belly with cool gel before placing the sonogram instrument on my skin. As I looked to the monitor trying to make sense out of the various shades of gray, I asked, "Well, doctor, is it Carolyn or Robert?"

"It's definitely Robert," she said, unaware of our hopes on the subject.

Immediately, my eyes filled as I looked at my daughter's face. I wanted more than anything to give her the gift of a sister, and I felt a loss for the little girl that I had imagined. The technician handed me a tissue as if it was second nature and Rich tried to appear sympathetic; however, he was beaming as if his team had just recruited the number-one draft pick.

Olivia stood perfectly still for a moment and then replied, "At least I don't have to share your jewelry with anyone when you die."

"Real nice thought for an eight-year-old," I whispered under my breath. I knew this was how Olivia handled disappointment: she finds a bright side and adds a hint of sarcasm.

Terese was at my side holding my hand as I gave birth to Bobby, formally Robert. It was a name Liz and I found fitting to go with William and John (Billy and Jack).

And yes, I did grow up wanting to be a Kennedy.

This time, while Billy and Jack waited at home with their aunt for the call, Terese helped me with my breathing, wiping the sweat and tears from my face. Rich anxiously paced the room while Olivia kept herself busy by checking the monitors and talking to whoever came within earshot. Sheila, one of my best friends since high school and my sister were both with us too. It was wonderful to share this special day with them.

The doctor predicted that the baby was in no hurry and suggested that everyone go for lunch and let me rest. Five minutes later, not even the epidural could mask the pain of the baby heading down the last of the birth canal. The doctor barely made it back in time. Terese held me tight while the girls called out encouragement. Rich held Olivia's hand, but she released herself from his grip and got right behind the doctor. When the baby's head crowned, the doctor asked if anyone wanted to touch it; we all declined, even Olivia. I pushed again and his shoulders released.

"Tricia, reach down and pull him out," the doctor said.

I leaned down, placed my swollen hands under his slippery little armpits, and pulled him out onto my stomach. There was not a dry eye in the room. Then, unexpectedly, the doctor handed Olivia the scissors.

"Okay, your turn."

Olivia turned to me and then to Rich with a big smile on her face. Then she climbed up onto the table and cut through the umbilical cord. Bobby exercised his lungs letting the world know he had arrived. The nurse took him from me, and Olivia and Rich stayed with him while she weighed him and cleaned him up. Terese stayed next to me as the doctor attended to my birthing aftermath. Rich was beaming as he laid our fourth child in my arms. I was at peace. He was so beautiful.

Terese's husband showed up and stayed with me for hours doting over his new godson. I do not remember missing my mother and father at this birth.

The next day I lay in my hospital bed holding my beautiful little boy in my arms. His hands were so little and perfect. Everything about him was perfect: the shape of his head, the size of his nose, the smell of his body. I fell deeply in love, again. I felt complete. Then I was startled by a ruckus in the hall that got closer and closer to my room.

"Billy, stop it! Olivia, leave him alone! Jack, get over here!" Rich hollered.

I looked back down at this incredible vision in my arms and whispered in his ear, "Welcome to our family. We are some bunch!"

🌱 🌱 🌱

"DAD, HOLD HIS HEAD; he needs support," I say, annoyed. His neck is not strong enough yet.

"Where did you get this baby? I do not remember this baby."

"I told you. You and Mom were in an accident, but you are okay now. I had that baby while you were in the hospital. Hold his head."

"The baby won't stop crying."

"Let me have him. He may be hungry."

I wake up to crying from the bassinet next to my bed. Half-awake, I reach in and take hold of the tiny infant yelling for me. I settle him to my breast and realize, once again, it was just a dream. "Shhh, shhh, you're okay," I say.

🌱 🌱 🌱

RICH BROUGHT IT UP right around our ninth wedding anniversary. Olivia was eight, Billy was six, Jack was four, and the baby was the perfect age, able to sit up and play but not run around or climb.

I protested. "I don't want to move to Los Angeles. I love it here. I have friends. I can't leave Terese."

"Tricia, it's a great opportunity for our family."

When I stood at the altar and professed my love for Rich in front of God and two hundred loved ones, we were both young and naive. We had no idea about the stresses marriage would bring us, or of the responsibilities of raising a family. All we knew was that we loved each other enough to think we could make it through anything. Now married nine years, on our third move, we had experienced plenty. And we were about to experience more.

Saying goodbye to Terese was like losing a limb. At first I played it off as if it were nothing. I pretended it would be like having two homes, as if I were just leaving for college. I focused on the fact that one of my best friends from high school, Mary Jane, lived in Los Angeles, as did Rich's younger sister Dorothy, whom I loved. I also focused on the fact that Sheila had just gotten word that her husband would also be relocating his work from San Francisco down south. Sheila and I had grown up together, both moved to California, and now would be moving together again. I would arrive with a village in place.

I left the entire process of finding a new home up to Rich. He bought a lovely place in a beautiful Santa Monica neighborhood about a mile and a half away from the beach.

"Don't cry, honey, you will love it in Los Angeles," Terese said.

"But you are family now! I don't want to lose any more family," I said.

"You won't lose me."

Terese knew this was a great opportunity for Rich and did her best to assure me that we would see one another often. The boys were young enough to be more excited about the pool at our new house than sad about leaving friends. Olivia had the hardest time with the change, so I did my best assuring her we'd make return visits. And I promised her a kitten.

PART THREE

SUPPORT

The human spirit has no idea what it can withstand until it is forced to lean on another.

CHAPTER 7

Let the Village Gather

It was August 2001 when we moved to LA. School would start soon, and we needed time to get settled. Leaving my comfort zone with Terese was difficult, but it was time.

I still held onto a lot of pain, but I had fewer bad dreams, smashed fewer windows, and my parents' death no longer occupied so many of my thoughts. I believed the pain held insight and guidance for me; I just had to be wise enough to find it. I considered myself happy, but being happy was different from actually declaring, "I will be happy. I am committed to being happy." I could change my world by looking at it differently. I decided to do this by making a conscious decision to be happy and embrace our move to Los Angeles.

Rich and I walked around our new house in disbelief as the events of September 11, 2001, unfolded. I cried hard watching the victims' friends and relatives grieve. For years, I had gotten accustomed to people telling me how they thought of me as soon as they experienced their own first big loss. That they had no idea how unbearable the pain could actually get. Yet, as I watched the human suffering from the comfort of my bedroom, I fully understood that I could not understand the magnitude of pain these relatives would experience, that there were losses that I could not fathom.

The national tragedy sank me into gloom, and certain phrases repeated in my head that I had heard over and over again with the loss of my parents. "Everything happens for a reason," is one that I hate. It drives wood under my fingernails. I do not know if people say it to comfort the person hurting or to make their own selves feel less vulnerable. I know they mean well. But, there is a reason? When I hear this, I wonder if God wants to yell, "I never said that!"

Then there is the expression "God only gives you what you can handle." Should I be flattered that God thought I could handle so much? Did I look like I could take on a lot, so he threw me a double? Obviously, many people get much more than they can handle.

Then there is the notion of karma, or "what goes around comes around." So, if something awful happens, you must have been a real asshole in a past life. How about just accepting that bad things happen to all kinds of people? Bad things happen. That's what I thought as I heard these clichés being offered to the newly grieving on television; you think you have your life planned, and then *bam*.

Not all things can be looked at from a positive point of view. Some things are simply awful and must be dealt with that way. But I kept my commitment to strive to be happy. I decided that if there were ways to look at things from a lighter, brighter point of view, I would.

Rich's career had been blossoming. Now, in the face of world upheaval, his new company stunned us by eliminating his position. We had just moved and taken on a big mortgage. The kids were enrolled in an expensive private school. Rich felt we would lose everything if he didn't secure a position instantly. He felt he was fighting the battle of a lifetime. I felt it was just a major inconvenience, and I was happy to be emotionally strong enough to keep both our spirits high. He had stood behind me in my grief; now it was my turn to be there for him. I kept reminding him, "Rich, we love each other. The kids are healthy, and we can do this."

His unemployment lasted over a year; it was challenging and humbling. We'd saved for the proverbial rainy day, so we were able to take time and find the right job. While he hunted, Rich had the opportunity to grow as a father. He took each of the children away on a trip alone for one-on-one bonding. My friends Sheila and Mary

Jane were a great support during this time, as was Dorothy, Rich's sister. Terese called often to check in on the kids, but more on me. She drove down for lunch one day and stayed the night. It wasn't the greatest year for our family, but there was so much to be grateful for and I tried to stay focused on that. Then Rich secured another position in Los Angeles and we were back on track.

🌲 🌲 🌲

I BEGAN MANY OF MY MORNINGS talking to Mary Jane after we carpooled our children safely to school. It was wonderful that we'd met thirty years ago in Pennsylvania and we now lived forty minutes apart in Los Angeles.

"I tried the back door last night. It did nothing for me," Mary Jane said.

"What! You tried the back door? What did you leverage?"

"Nothing, I just did it."

Mary Jane had been married for more than twenty years. She struggled with her marriage and with finding excitement in her life. "You gave up the back door without leveraging anything? You are supposed to get a piece of jewelry or a new car or a vacation out of it. Something! Anything! Mary Jane, the back door is not supposed to be free," I said. "You know what you need? You need to visit the Love Boutique, and we need to get some excitement back into your life."

"The Love Boutique?" she questioned.

"There is one on Wilshire. I have never been there, but I'm sure they can help."

Two days later, Mary Jane drove down to Santa Monica and we ventured out to the Love Boutique. As we entered, everything appeared pretty calm. We headed to the back, figuring things would pop up there and, indeed, they did. The whole wall was covered from top to bottom in toys. Some looked like rabbit ears, some looked like rocket ships, and some looked like the king of the jungle.

"Hi, can I help you find anything?" a salesgirl said in a squeaky whisper. I was taken aback by her voice.

"No thank you, we're just looking," Mary Jane quickly replied.

"She's so full of shit," I said. "She's a frustrated forty-three-year-old going through a midlife crisis, and we need to jump-start her sexuality before it's completely dead."

Mary Jane shot me a look.

"I love you, Mary Jane," I said.

"This one here helps you locate your G-spot," the salesgirl whispered. "It's meant to stimulate you externally and internally at the same time."

"Oh no, don't tell me that is what I think it is," Mary Jane said, pointing to a replica of the male private parts connected to a belt.

The salesgirl walked over to the shelf and removed a thick black belt with a rubber penis attached. "This is a strap-on. Two women use it, but heterosexual couples like to use it too. It gives the woman control."

I had a frightening visual of Rich and me in the bedroom and me wearing a strap-on.

"Oh, that's just not right," I muttered, trying to shake the thought from my mind.

I left them alone in women wonderland and made my way to the book section, saying, "She will need something to stimulate her mind as well."

I walked over to the bookshelf and examined the covers. "Are there any books about the women being in control?" I asked. "I like to fantasize about being a college professor and my male students will do anything to get their grades up."

The girl walked over and picked a book off the shelf for me. "Try this one, erotica written for women."

I spotted a book facing out with the title *All You Need to Know About Performing Fellatio*. "How in the hell could there be a book over three hundred pages long about a blow job?"

"I would rather get a manicure and pedicure," Mary Jane said.

"But a manicure and pedicure only last about two weeks. We are trying to give you a lifetime of feeling good about yourself as a woman, remember. I'm buying this book," I said, holding the guide to fellatio in my hands. "I think my skill level could use some enhancing," I admitted.

"You have to be kidding."

As we left the store, Mary Jane gave me a hard time about my purchase.

"I can't believe you bought that book. You really like sex that much?"

"Sometimes, but not always. Look, Mary Jane. I'm serious. Good marriages don't just happen. I have four kids and I'm exhausted most of the time, but I want to feel sexy and I also want Rich to feel good. Just the fact that I bought the book will make Rich feel thrilled. It has nothing to do with my sex drive. Mine is as low as yours. But I want my marriage to work for mine and Rich's sake, and the children's. I know sex is really important in the marriage, so I try to do my best. And Mary Jane...tell the truth, you're interested in what my book says, aren't you?"

She made an attempt to push me, but I ducked.

🌱 🌱 🌱

ONE SATURDAY AFTERNOON not long after we moved to LA, while I ferried various children on numerous missions, Rich drove Billy to a birthday party for his new best buddy, Byron, who happened to be the son of Barbara Lazaroff, a well-known restaurant designer and philanthropist, and her husband, Wolfgang Puck, the famous chef.

"I've never been to a Halloween birthday party like this one before," he told me. "The backyard was turned into a small carnival. There were exotic birds, monkeys, clowns, jumpy-jumps, and games. There was a haunted house with live characters dressed as ghosts and monsters. Byron's mom was wearing a Wonder Woman costume."

"Shit," I said. "I wish I'd gone."

The following week, Billy wanted to take Byron fencing, so I called the house asking for Barbara.

"Hi, I'm Tricia, Billy's mom," I said. "We'd like to take Byron fencing with us today."

"That would be fine." She was neither aloof nor overly friendly.

An hour later, we headed out to pick up Byron. The house was a big, beautiful English Tudor. I drove up to the unique iron gate and pressed the call button. After I drove through the gate and parked, I walked past the carefully tended lawn to the front door and knocked. A man with a white ponytail opened the door. His smile was warm and welcoming. "Hi, I'm Barbara's father. I'll get Byron."

I stood in the foyer—it was definitely different. Immediately, I thought about what I would tell Terese. Although the house was old and charming, everything in it was modern and bold. Color was everywhere. Individuality was everywhere. I saw endless photographs. There were two tables, one against the wall to the left and one located directly under the staircase. Both were covered with pictures. I tried to get a look at some of them, but did not want to get caught snooping. Bright, colorful artwork was everywhere. Every inch of wall was covered. I heard birds squawking, "*Barbara! Barbara! Byron!*"

Mary Jane told me she'd read in a magazine that they kept llamas in the backyard, along with parrots and huge tortoises, but I couldn't see anything out of the ordinary from where I stood. Byron came down the steps and off we went.

A month passed without another word, and then Byron's mom called to tell me she had filed for divorce.

"I waited to do it at the holiday," she said, "so the boys wouldn't be in school and there'd be less press. Since Billy and Byron play together a lot, I wanted you to understand."

"Oh..." What does one say on that occasion? "I'm sorry."

"Yes, so am I, mostly for the boys."

We spoke for a minute or two, and I was impressed that during this painful time in her life, knowing how close Billy and Byron had become, she cared that I understood why she had not been more available.

I did not hear from her for many months, and then she called the house one night.

"I wanted to talk to you about a situation that arose with Byron and another boy at school, since he and Billy often play together," she said. "Do you have a minute?"

"Sure."

We spoke for a bit about common playground politics and the best way to teach our boys to handle them. I appreciated her insight, since Byron had an older brother and she had experience with boys, and shared mine. The conversation was insightful and comfortable.

"Hm." She contemplated that for a moment and then said, "I'd like to invite you and your husband to an art showing I've sponsored tomorrow night at the La Brea Tar Pits. Are you available?"

🌱 🌱 🌱

RICH AND I ARRIVED at the museum on a perfect Los Angeles evening, all warm air and clear skies. The exhibit consisted of artist Steve Tobin's monumental bronze sculptures that had been cast from animal bones, tree roots, and termite hills. Pieces were arranged among the museum's art in the gardens and the center hall of the museum. Waitstaff dressed in black and white walked around with silver trays in their hands offering delicious bite-sized hors d'oeuvres. The crowd was an eclectic mix of ages and styles; some people were dressed casually, others elegantly, but most were sleek or funky, what one would expect from an LA crowd at an art showing.

Barbara entered the gallery surrounded by a crowd of people, laughing, shaking hands with her guests. Her presence thundered. She struck me as a piece of art herself—something Picasso might have conjured up when he was feeling passionate. Her thick, long, black hair framed the structure of her face. Her cheekbones sat high. Her lips were full and brightly painted; her nose, perfect. It was her eyes, big and brown, that captivated her audience. Her outfit was stunning: flowing fabric in deep shades of burgundy with hints of purple, with a drape of silk that led from her right shoulder to her waist. It was elegant and refined, yet sexy, showing off her curves. Her amethyst jewelry offset the dress perfectly, and I realized I was a bit starstruck and intrigued as I watched her work the crowd.

"She's gorgeous," I said, poking Rich.

"Yeah, but you're prettier."

"You'll say anything to get laid."

She took the podium and spoke graciously about how good the city of Los Angeles had been to her, and what a joy it was to bring Tobin's art in from the East Coast, and what an impact he had made on the art world. Rich and I walked through the gallery and outside exhibit, making our way to the open bar. Waiting for a cocktail, I felt a light touch on my arm.

"Hello, thank you for coming," Barbara said. She was even more glamorous up close.

"Hi, I'm Billy's mom. We spoke last night."

"Yes, of course. How's Los Angeles treating your family? It's a different city from San Francisco and a big place to be bringing up four children."

"We're doing great, thank you for asking."

She looked straight into my eyes and for that instant made me feel like the guest of honor. *This is her secret*, I thought. *She makes everyone feel special and respected.*

A young man walked over and whispered something to her, and she said, "Excuse me, I'm needed up front."

I was taken by her delicate, feminine manner accompanied by strength and confidence. She appeared genuine and caring, yet exuded power and control.

Not long after the art show, the children had their annual Olympics Day at school, with all the students representing different countries. It was a wonderful small private school located in West Hollywood that prided itself on diversity. It did not matter if your child was attending on a full scholarship or if you were some big Hollywood hotshot; all anyone cared about was the children. The parents set up camp on the field, and the day turned into a big picnic. Leeza Gibbons, whom I recognized from television, had a son in Olivia's class. She knew I was new to the school and had made an effort to make me feel welcomed. We spoke for a bit, and then I went and set up camp.

Barbara waltzed onto the field in bright colors and a big red hat wide enough to provide shade for her and anyone within ten feet of her. She wore fancy beaded sandals and had perfectly pedicured fuchsia toes. She wore white jeans with printed pink and red roses, and a long sleeved silk fuchsia top. I sat under my umbrella there in my gray tank shirt and white overall shorts, thinking about how much money someone would have to pay me to have the balls to wear an outfit like that to a kids' field day.

"Hello!" I called.

"Well, you look ready and armed."

"I look ready for the barn? Why, because I'm wearing overalls?"

"I said you looked ready and *armed*, for the weather."

"Yes. Everyone's treating it like the news story of the year: 'LA Weather Uncomfortable.'" I patted an empty beach chair next to mine. "Do you need some shade?

You can hide in here for a while."

"I'd love some shade. That's what the huge hat is for." She sat down with a big sigh.

to do?"

"Excuse me?" She looked confused.

"Just now I called to check if I had any new messages. A recording came on and said my mailbox was almost full and I should remove all unnecessary messages. I have kids yelling at me all day long, then a husband who periodically forgets that I don't work for him. And now my cellphone's telling me what to do? I don't think so!"

"I have never had that happen, but I can see why it would be frustrating," she said.

"You know what else I hate? I hate when I use spell check and the computer says, 'no suggestions,' like I spell so badly it can't even make a guess."

Barbara smiled without saying anything.

"I guess you never had that happen to you either?"

She giggled but then started laughing a little too much.

"It really wasn't that funny," I said.

"Sorry," she said, covering her mouth. "Actually it was; you're funny."

We spoke about the weather and the children, but then it was time. Ten minutes had passed, and I needed to talk about my parents. Not for her sympathy. Just because it's the second most important thing to know about me. The most important thing, she already knew: I was happily married with four babies. "Did you know my parents were killed in a car accident?"

"Yes, I did," she answered softly.

So, Billy had told Byron about his grandparents.

"I have lost people close to me," she said, "but never a family member. My dearest friend is very sick right now. She has cancer, bladder cancer. I'm beside myself. I go to the hospital every day; and at night once the boys are settled, I massage her, I clean her, and I sleep there. I do whatever she needs but I feel so helpless. I can't imagine losing her."

Barbara paused for a moment and then continued. "How do you move forward?"

"Some things are changed forever, but I made a conscious decision to be happy again, and I am."

"You can be happy with so much pain in your life?" she asked. "It's hard to imagine. Are you religious?"

"I stopped praying when my parents died. Although, once when Bobby was really sick, I begged for God's help. Does that make me a hypocrite?"

Her expression changed from compassion to worry. "What about your parents? Do you talk to them?"

"No, it just doesn't work for me. But I try to use the pain, and the lessons I have learned from the accident, to be a better person. I had to work at finding happiness and look at my world differently. Otherwise the pain and anger would have destroyed me."

It had been a while, but I felt the need to break something. How did this conversation go from zero to a hundred? I started it but I'd never met someone with the courage to continue it. I looked around, not finding a window in sight. I dug my fingernails into the side of my leg, flinching as the pain intensified. Only my sister Liz knew about my smashing windows in my mind. I never told Terese. When I finally got the nerve to confess to my sister, she looked at me with relief on her face and said, "I cock a gun in my head."

"Are you happy?" I asked Barbara.

"I'm working on it. Both of my parents are still alive, but the betrayal and divorce negotiations were hard; I feel my children's pain. And I'm consumed with the likelihood of losing my friend, because she has two daughters and they just lost their father, and all of this has been happening at the same time."

Olivia ran over to us, calling, "Mom, hurry! My race is about to start."

Barbara joined me with the rest of the fifth-grade parents at the finish line, all of us armed with our camcorders to capture the event. Olivia flew out of the starting gate and had the lead until she tripped and hit the ground like a football player getting tackled.

"Get up, baby, get up!" I yelled. She looked over to me and got up. "Run!"

Olivia started back down the track, finishing last. I went over to hug her, but she pushed me away, fighting back tears. Her friends quickly surrounded her, so I gave her space and went to watch Billy compete in the softball throw. I saw Barbara talking to some of the first-grade parents, but I gave her space. As noon approached, we all took a break for lunch. As I pulled out Olivia's and Billy's deli sandwiches, Barbara and Byron sat down with us.

"Has Olivia recovered?" Barbara asked quietly, so Olivia would not hear.

"Yeah." I winced. "Childhood mishaps build confidence. Plus, I got it on video and I'm going to show it at her wedding."

Photo Gallery

My mother. I found this picture, very worn out, in my father's wallet after the accident.

My parents at our wedding

My family on Christmas Eve, when big hair was in style.

Olivia and I, weeks before the accident, when all was complete.

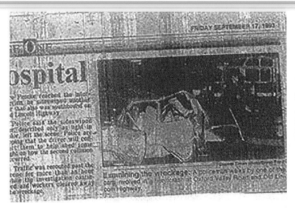

The accident. It's unbelievable that Julianne made it out with only minor injuries.

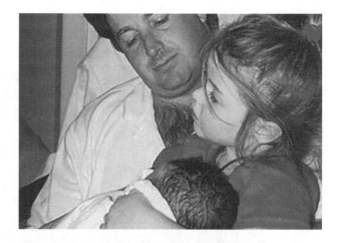

Olivia holding baby Jack, minutes after he was born.

Vanessa with Jack at his baptism.

Terese and I

All the grandchildren before Bobby was born.

Terese back in her professional working period with her mentor.

Moving to Los Angeles

Barbara at Spago

Barbara and I

Rich and I out on New Year's Eve with Terese and Robert.

Family

Circle of Love

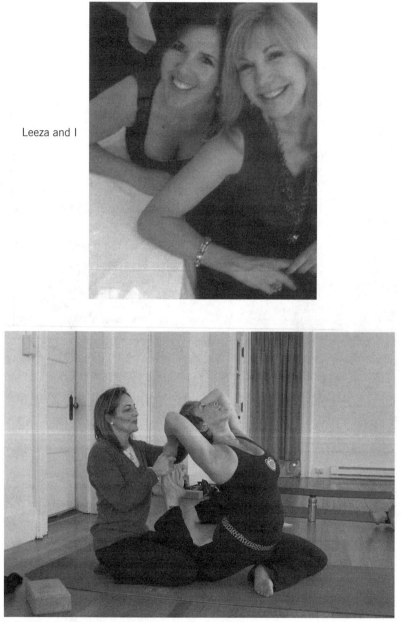

Leeza and I

Julie assisting Terri in a yoga pose.

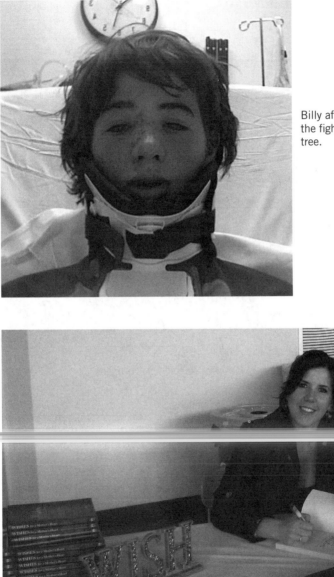

Billy after losing the fight with the tree.

Signing books for *Wishes for a Mother's Heart*.

A CAHNERS PUBLICATION

american baby

FOR EXPECTANT AND NEW PARENTS · SEPTEMBER 1995

Smart New Looks for Kids

Parents' Guide to Vaccines

Making Your Home Baby-Safe

Silly Faces!
Contest Winners

Olivia appearing on a magazine cover. Olivia's photo was used five years later. Unfortunately, my parents weren't alive to see it.

Sheila, Mary Jane, and I, out having fun.

My mother's paintings. She was in the process of finishing the large one when she was killed. It was the last gift she gave me, which I found in her studio after the accident. It was a beautiful surprise.

Jack's creation of Martha. The snakes signify danger, the thorns at her feet signify protection, and the doves in her branches signify maternal love.

Dr. Julianne graduating from medical school. She is currently working on her fellowship in Hematology/Oncology.

Olivia and Aunt Dorothy. I told Martha one day we will have a Red Tent party for Olivia, which we did. It was a wonderful celebration with about thirty adult women and six young girls.

My sister Liz and I

(Top) Our family all grown up

(Left) Sweet Aaron

Martha changing outfits

CHAPTER 8

Barbara's Big Love

Barbara became a source of love and security in my life. Billy and Byron played together all the time, so we spent a lot of time together. My children jumped right on board, embracing her love as if it had been there forever. I never took a moment for granted. She took Olivia shopping, talked to Jack in detail about his art, and held Bobby on her lap and invited him to sleep over and eat ice cream in bed. I called Byron the fifth LaVoice child, and Barbara teased that Billy was one of her own. She was only nine years older than me, but her maternal love was so strong and the void I felt was so deep—my longing for the love of my mother, my children's grandmother. Barbara had no idea what she meant to us, because she always went about her life touching the lives of others with poise and grace.

Rich and I sat in the den talking about our lives in Los Angeles and how we thought the kids were adapting. I was happy to be having such a frank talk with him and felt safe saying, "I think maybe my mother sent Barbara to me."

"Why's that?"

"It's like with Terese...it feels like she's been here forever. She's so loving with me, the kids and you too. How can someone who's known me for so little time care so deeply about my life? Maybe my mom sent them to look after me. Does that sound crazy?"

"No, Tricia, it sounds nice."

🌱 🌱 🌱

SPAGO WAS BARBARA AND WOLFGANG'S flagship restaurant on North Canon Drive in the heart of Beverly Hills. Wolfgang came from a small town in Austria. Barbara grew up in a working-class neighborhood in the Bronx throughout most of her childhood, then in Queens, and then a short time in Long Island. Together they opened Spago and created the Wolfgang Puck brand. Wolfgang cooked. Barbara designed and handled marketing and publicity. They both greeted guests and shared business tasks. I had read a quote in a *People* magazine article stating that Wolfgang had always been a great chef but Barbara kicked the restaurants into high gear.

Other parents at the school spoke highly about Barbara's hard work, working around the clock designing and building their restaurants. Once she became a mother, she flew back and forth between LA and other cities when building and opening restaurants. I knew she was one of the first to design an open kitchen in an upscale restaurant, turning the kitchen into a stage that allowed patrons to witness Wolfgang creating edible masterpieces, and I wondered if her design was the origin for the elevation of many celebrity chefs.

A group of us began meeting at Spago each week for what Barbara called "Power Lunch Friday." I called it "Friday Cleavage Lunch," and I looked forward to these events. The kids were in school, and I could be one of the girls with the other regulars.

I had come to accept that in Los Angeles, breasts are fashion accessories, so I put on a little blue dress that hugged my curves and plunged in the front. I drove my blue Sequoia mom mobile down Wilshire Boulevard past the Hilton and crossed Santa Monica Boulevard to the stretch of Wilshire that meets Rodeo Drive. Tourists from all over the world crowded the street, enjoying a perfect LA day. I pulled the curlers from my hair while waiting at the Beverly Drive intersection, turned the corner onto Canon, and pulled over to apply my makeup before pulling up to the valet.

"Welcome," he said.

When he opened the door, an empty Starbucks cup fell to the ground. He picked it up and held on to it. I tossed the curlers onto the passenger seat and reached down to place my shoes on my feet.

The moment I entered the restaurant, I could feel my whole body relax. Friday Cleavage Lunch: leave your troubles at the door and come to love, laugh, and savor a fabulous meal. There was nowhere else I would rather be at that moment.

The hostess greeted me. "Hi, everyone's here. Come, I'll show you to the table."

"Am I okay?" I asked. "I did my hair and makeup in the car." I'd been showing up for Cleavage Lunch for months. She was used to it.

She discreetly dabbed my left cheek with her thumb. The smell of fresh flowers blew in from the patio. Bold colors, art, the sun bursting through the colorful artisan glass windows, the lush fabric of the chairs—it was all Barbara's design. Her soul could be felt within the restaurant walls and beyond in the open-air garden with its beautiful old olive trees, sculpted fountains, and cascading waterfall. Her passion for life and her need to love and be loved could be felt everywhere. The staff, the patrons, even the paint on the walls radiated unique energy. From A-list actresses and Hollywood mucky-mucks to Friday regulars and tourists—every guest was treated like a close friend who had been gone too long and there were always new people to meet.

"Honey, come here. Meet my friends," I heard Barbara call once she spotted me. "This is my darling friend Trish. Trish, remember I told you about Maude and George, who just celebrated their fifty-fifth wedding anniversary?"

I smiled and nodded. Then we were off to the next table, a group of women. "This is my Irish Catholic friend Trish. The one I told you about with all the kids," she announced.

"Only four, Barbara. I'm not a farm animal." We walked to another table, and again there were kisses and introductions.

"Margaret's daughter is the one who I told you about making beautiful furniture." Next table: "Remember I told you Chuck was on the beach when the tidal wave hit?" He reached up and held tight onto her hand. Next table: Barbara leaned over and kissed the woman on the cheek. "This is Suzy. Remember I told you about my friend who just celebrated her fifth year free of lung cancer?"

I felt like I was at a family reunion and walking around with a favorite aunt. I would act as if I remembered everything she had told me about everyone. Eventually, I broke free and told her I would meet her at the table. "Go ahead, honey. I'll be right over," she said as she went back to giving her heart and soul.

I approached the table, and my heart warmed in a mother's embrace. I was home, safe, understood, loved here at this table. I loved who I was with these women, and I loved how they perceived me. Except for one, they were all about ten years older than I, and all very committed mothers. Most of them I had met through Barbara. There was Veronica, the sexy Italian beauty who lived for love and passion; Caroline, the funniest, most talented woman in Hollywood, who gave up her career as an actress to stay home with her children; Chloe, sweet and kind, who was always exploding with creative ideas; Sara, a classic beautiful redhead whose laugh warmed my heart every time I heard it; and Raquel, a year younger than I, who worked very hard at her job and single parenting. I wondered if she got the same maternal love from this group of women as I did. The simple terms of endearment—"Honey, did you have a good night? Sweetheart, did you change your hair?"—provided me with such strength. I felt replenished every time I was with this group, and it gave me the ability to go back to Rich and the kids and be that much more loving to them. These women had lived a lot of life. They knew pain, birth, death, betrayal, and trust. However, more important, they knew love.

"Good afternoon, you nutty wonderful bitches," I said as I approached them.

"Hey, our girl is here!" Veronica announced, reaching her arms out to me.

I walked around the table kissing all of them, first on one cheek and then the other as if I had studied some foreign-film etiquette.

"Hey, sweetie, how are you?" Sara said as she squeezed my hand.

"I love your bracelet," Chloe said as I approached her.

"Thank you. It's fake and so is my tan. I got it from a salon, and my nails I got from the beauty parlor. My cleavage, I got from a Victoria Secret bra," I said. "I love your blouse."

I was happy to see two empty seats next to Caroline. I would take one and Barbara the other. I sat down and Caroline gave me her usual greeting, "Hey, love of my life, why are you so late?"

"I was home wiping snot off of children's faces and playing my husband's flute. Do you think I get to come to these lunches without paying the piper first?"

"I don't get it."

"Playing the flute—blowing his horn."

"You just serviced your husband?"

"Caroline. It's the middle of the day. He's at work. The kids are at school. It was just fun to say."

"Maybe if you service him more often, he'll give you some money for a decent pair of shoes."

"Hey, discount retail. Twenty bucks," I defended.

Barbara walked up, and I moved my purse from the chair next to me so she could sit. Barbara was always so busy at these lunches. She checked in with us periodically but never rested until dessert was served. The waiter served slices of smoked-salmon-and-caviar pizza as I searched my purse for reading glasses. I held them to my eyes, not willing to commit to putting them on. Barbara enjoyed the fact that, although she was nine years older than I was, she could still see without glasses.

"Do you want me to order something for you?" she asked.

"No, you'll order something healthy and I won't eat it. I'm getting a cheeseburger."

"Try something different. What about sautéed Maine swordfish with caramelized sweet white corn, littleneck clams, marjoram, garlic potato purée, Spanish chorizo, and parsley clam broth?"

"What? Are you doing an infomercial?"

"Grilled prime ribeye steak with Swiss chard, thyme, Armagnac green-peppercorn sauce, and *pommes aligot*?"

"I'm getting a cheeseburger and, let me guess, you are getting a plate of beets? I need the iron, Miss Boring. And it's a sirloin burger."

The waiter took our orders. Barbara placed one hand on his arm and the other on his back. "Could you please bring some of the white corn agnolotti with truffles for the table to try? Thank you."

I reached for my third piece of bread and gestured to Chloe to pass the butter across from her.

"You don't need butter. You're going to ruin your lunch," Barbara scolded.

I ignored her. When I first started coming to lunches, I ate very little of my meal so I could give Rich my leftovers. Barbara hated that I did this and started ordering food for me to take home to him. I tried to carry my doggie bag out quietly. I think I'm the only person who gets a doggie bag from Spago.

Barbara got up to greet more guests, and our meals were served. I surveyed the table: all exotic salads, except for Barbara's beet-and-goat-cheese concoction and my cheeseburger. When the restaurant started to empty, Sherry Yard, the head pastry chef, walked up, wearing her cotton-candy-pink chef coat dappled with batter and a bit of chocolate. She was adorable; her hair changed color every time I saw her. Today, it was a vibrant red. She was trailed by several of the waitstaff, all carrying something decadent in each hand. Chocolate this, apple that, banana something—it was endless.

At every lunch, I would listen to the girls order salads—or "Hold the potatoes" or "Pass the Splenda"—but Sherry's desserts were always devoured. Sherry took the plates, one by one, and placed them in the middle of the table, and the aroma of fresh-baked vanilla, nutmeg, and chocolate teased our senses. The presentation was always as impressive as the flavors. Sherry gave us a brief description of each dish and asked us for our opinion on a new blackberry tart. The spoons flew.

🌳 🌳 🌳

I KNEW BARBARA WAS HURTING over her divorce, explaining to her boys, and she didn't like fighting over what she had worked so hard to create. I tried to be a good listener and offer her a place to vent as someone new to the scene.

"Everyone gets through the pain differently," I told her as we sat on a bench, watching as the boys ran around the soccer field. "I break glass with my imagination when I'm hurting. I have broken hundreds, probably hundreds of thousands, of windows since the accident. I could be laughing at a party, talking to a group of people, and smashing the windows over their heads without missing a beat. Teacher conferences, doctors' offices, home—I smash window after window. Sometimes I side-kick. On better days, I just put my fist through it."

"Tricia, talk to me about your mother. I would love to know her better."

"It's hard for me to talk about her, still now, after all these years. My brain has stored it away, but it's also hard to describe her. I realized the other night after the opera that I can tell you a thousand things my father said to me, but very few that my mother told me. She was the love, the trust, the strength. I walked in her shadow my whole childhood, and then as I grew, she walked in mine. We were very connected. There was nothing I could not say to my mother. I always had great trust in her. Don't get me wrong. She disciplined us, but it was always in a very loving, gentle way, and she never criticized us—or anyone else for that matter. She just loved her girls and supported us. I truly don't remember ever being mad at her, except one time in eighth grade when she made me come home by 8:30 and my friends were still allowed out. I usually got my way with her. A little pleading went a long way. If I shed a tear, the world was mine."

I realized I was twirling the bracelets on Barbara's wrist as I spoke, like you'd see a child do in church.

"Everyone who knew her loved her. She was beautiful, but frail. We worried about her a lot. She got sick often and seemed to need a lot of rest. I don't know why, but we were all always worrying about her. Maybe that's just the way it is with moms." I paused. "I know it must seem like I should have gotten over it by now, but I don't think a day will go by that I don't wish she were here with us right now, sitting having tea. There is no explanation for the loss, and time does not heal all wounds."

Barbara reached over and cupped her hand to my face. She held her hand on my cheek, having no idea how many times my mother had held me in this same way.

🌱 🌱 🌱

"GOOD MORNING, SUNSHINE!"

We had a new ritual: whoever called first would start the conversation this way as a reminder that life can be what we make of it.

"What the hell are you doing up so early?" I asked.

"That's my morning greeting?"

"Sorry," I said. "Good morning, sunshine. I woke up in a mood and can't shake it. I need something, like a cigarette or something sweet to eat. Relax. I haven't smoked a cigarette in twenty-five years. I just meant I need something emotionally gratifying, like a chocolate sundae."

"Honey, it's your hormones. I told you, you're perimenopausal."

I rolled my eyes, but said nothing into the phone.

"How's this for emotionally fulfilling? I love you. You are sweet and wonderful. Now shake it off, go for a walk, or do some leg lifts. I'm here for you all day."

I loved how comfortable Barbara was at expressing her love and how comfortable I had become at receiving it. Why had I never thought of something so obvious and simple myself? A million times, I had heard a girlfriend say, "Oh, I just need to eat something" or "I need a drink." I wish I had thought to say, "I love you. You're perfect. Now, do you need to feed your fat ass?"

Of course, all of my terms of endearment would need to be followed by sarcasm in fear of too much intimacy. How well the human spirit responds to love, but how hard it is for so many of us to express it. Barbara always kissed me hello and goodbye and never would leave me without hollering out the door a "love you." She used more terms of endearment in one conversation than I would use in a month.

But Veronica was the greatest at expressing love, and helped me greatly with how to say "I love you" to people—not just "love you." Adding that "I" makes it a bit more intimate and awkward. It was hard for me at first, but now I'm really good at saying "I love you" to everyone I love.

Barbara and the other women inspired me to try harder to be more verbally expressive with my love. I began to say "I love you" to friends I had known forever but to whom I had never said it before. At first, I would just throw it out there. "Talk to you soon. Love you." Then I became more aware and began saying it when a friend was hurting, and made sure to pause and say it like I meant it: "I love you." It was hard at first, but it made me feel so good. The first time I told Mary Jane I loved her, I could tell she was uncomfortable, yet touched.

I once knew a girl named Love. Well, I never met her personally, but I did some business with her over the phone. It was interesting because every time I said her name, I felt good. It must be wonderful to have been brought up with everyone calling you Love.

🌿 🌿 🌿

BARBARA HAD TOLD ME that, in a million years, she never thought she and Wolfgang would split up. They had been married almost twenty years and together almost five before that. Now he was with a woman the restaurant had hired as a hostess.

"I tried, Tricia, I really did. For the kids' sake, I forgave and forgave, but enough was enough. I had to file."

Now she worried very much about how it all would affect her boys. As she and Wolfgang sorted out details, I could see her wanting to move on. She had met a nice guy and was working hard on some great projects but her thoughts were consumed with the divorce. I tried to help, but never felt my words or company brought her any solace. One day, she quoted something she'd read: "'You cannot beat an enemy who has an outpost in your head.' I'm working on that."

I loved that, and I loved that she would share it with me, but I hated to see her so low. I wanted to do something. It never left my mind how Terese had so beautifully used the gardenias as symbolism that night to represent the years of my parents' passing. I had something really important to convey to Barbara, so one Sunday evening, I picked up some art supplies and ventured over to Barbara's house. She was in her robe and slippers when I got there. I could hear the boys upstairs carrying on about a football game.

"What are we doing?" she asked. "Making pictures? Decorating frames?"

"Just wait."

We walked through the narrow hall to the kitchen, and she sat in her purple fuzzy robe with her elbows propped and her hands holding her chin. I took five small bowls from the cupboard and placed them in a line on the wooden kitchen table in front of her.

"Are we scrapbooking?" she went on, ignoring my request.

"Just wait a second! You are worse than Bobby."

I took five small bags of colored sand from the first bag, then placed two larger bowls on the counter behind with the second bag. I pulled a beautiful glass bottle about eight inches high from the third bag and placed it directly in front of her.

"Oh, fun, sand art," she said.

"You don't know. Could you be any more childlike with your impatience? We aren't making sand art," I said. "We are reorganizing your thoughts."

Now she shot me a look.

"This bottle represents your head. The sand represents different things in your life. You are going to fill the bottle with what you feel is worthy and deserving of your attention and emotional energy. Okay?"

"Okay," she replied.

"However, only fill the bottle three-fourths of the way. The last quarter is mine." She perked right up like a child in front of finger paints for the first time.

"Okay, I'm ready." She examined the bottle and then placed it in front of her.

"Now, tell me what is important to you."

"My boys, Cameron and Byron, of course."

"Okay, pick a color that represents your boys."

She studied the five colors in front of her and went with the blue. I placed a plastic funnel in the mouth of the bottle, and she guided the blue sand into the base of the bottle.

"Okay, what's next?"

"Well," I said, "what's important to you?"

"Family. But first let me put another spoonful of blue sand in."

"Pick another color for your family."

"White, but since my boys are my family too, I'm going to add some blue to the white."

"Go, girlfriend. It's your head."

She smiled and sifted in a large scoop of white and blue sand to represent the time and love she felt for her family. Red depicted how she felt for her new love, John. She chose pink to represent her friendships and yellow to represent her work. Three-fourths filled, the bottle sat in front of us representing all of the people and things worthy of Barbara's attention and emotion. "Now what?"

"My turn," I said, as Byron walked into the kitchen.

"What are you two doing?" he asked.

"We're prioritizing my brain," Barbara joked.

"What?" Byron blinked.

"Every person has only so much room in their heads to focus on things," I said. "Psychologists call it 'attentional resources.' So you need to decide what is important to you and what is most deserving of your attention. The same is true with emotions: each person can give emotion to so many things. The sand represents the things in your mother's life that she chooses to give her attention and emotions to." I reached into the big bag and pulled out two more colors: purple and an ugly yellowish brown.

"I get to name these two, but you decide how much sand to use." I poured purple sand into a big bowl. "What do you think this represents?"

"That's Mom," Byron said. "Purple is her favorite color."

"I agree." She smiled. "It's me."

"And what do you think this ugly brown represents?" I asked, pouring a bowlful.

"All the crap in my life."

There was no need to elaborate. I got right in her face and took her hands in mine. Aware of Byron's presence, I said very seriously, "Fill the rest of the bottle, Barbara, brown sand first, and then the purple. But remember, whatever space the brown sand uses means there is that much less room for the purple."

She straightened her back up and tucked her legs under herself, leaning in towards the table. Tightening her lips, she shook her head as she reached for the bowl of brown sand.

"Well, it would be silly for me to pretend that I'm not going to give this some of my attention and emotion..."

Byron and I sat quietly, as if our silence offered her some privacy. She paused and stared at the brilliant colors of red, pink, white, blue, and yellow. I wondered what she was thinking. No one spoke as she scooped her spoon into the bowl of brown sand that stood for all of the misery in her life.

"Just one good-sized scoop—that is all I'm going to give it." She lowered the sand into the funnel and we all watched as the ugly brown sand tainted her perfect rainbow-filled vase.

"There," she said, a big, beautiful smile on her face. Then, with both hands, she dug right into the center of the purple bowl of sand. "Could someone please move the funnel?"

Byron pulled the funnel from the bottle, and she filled the bottle with her own hands until purple sand reached the top, spilling out all over the table.

"Oh, it's beautiful." She held the bottle high.

As I swished the excess purple sand back into the bowl, Byron wandered back up the stairs. Barbara kissed my cheek and placed her sand bottle on the kitchen windowpane overlooking the front gardens.

CHAPTER 9

Full with Everything

When schedules allowed, my wonderful circle of love would meet for Friday Cleavage Lunches. Leeza joined us when her busy life allowed and always sent me home with a desperately needed bit of wisdom. Life had gotten a little busy around our house, and I was doing my best. My cousin's daughter, Vanessa, was living with us in hopes of turning her life around after a few tough teenage years. She was a great kid and deserved every chance we could give her, and she was the best mother's helper I could ever ask for. However, she needed guidance and had to adjust to the rules I set around the house.

And then my nephew Aaron asked to come across the country and live with us while attending college. He had gotten into some trouble with drugs and was also looking for a chance to turn his life around. While he stayed with us, he was a good kid, he did very well in school, was an excellent soccer player, and was very well liked by his friends. But Aaron was so damaged that I felt lost about how to help him. He ruminated so much about life, I could understand how he turned to drugs to turn off his mind. Many times, I would walk into a room and find him just sitting there in silence, thinking. When I talked to him, I bumped into walls he put up everywhere: around love, his anger towards God, and his notion that we all just die in the end. I was prevented from reaching him in any way.

Liz tried desperately to get him help, but he did not respond well to it. Everyone was hoping his time with us would make a difference, but I did not see it happening. He seemed permanently damaged.

He had been just a child, nine years old, at the time of my parent's accident. He loved his mother and father, but his grandparents were a huge part of his life. They were such a source of love, confidence, and safety for him. When they were killed so suddenly I don't think his fragile, innocent mind knew what to do. The pain was just way too much for this sensitive, overthinking little boy; the realization that life can change in a phone call, that people you love with all your heart can be taken from you and be gone forever. So, he built walls and found a way to numb the pain.

At eighteen, he was searching for a new chance in life, but he also desperately was searching for relief from the pain within his thoughts and heart. It broke my heart to witness such suffering. I tried and tried to say something to make him feel better but did not feel like I was doing much good.

🌳 🌳 🌳

IT WAS A LOT, a full house, so when I had the chance to meet with my friends, I grabbed it. Their love and support was vital, rejuvenating me so I could go home and give the love needed there.

I walked into Spago and greeted the hostess.

"I'm going to use the ladies' room first," I said, but the hostess came flying after me.

"Tag!" she whispered. "You have a tag hanging out of your jacket."

"I know. I like to keep them on long enough to show Barbara and the other women how much I saved, but thank you."

Barbara spotted me. "Honey, honey. Over here."

I was delighted to see Barbara's beautiful mother, Ellie, having lunch with a friend. I had become close to Ellie. She understood my pain; like Terese, she'd lost her mother at the tender age of four. She played an important role in my mothering, offering me advice that I took so deeply to heart.

I walked over to the table and kissed Ellie hello. Barbara reached down and plucked the tag from my jacket.

"Check out the savings," I whispered.

She quickly glanced at it and shook her head. "I need to go upstairs and meet with the accountant for a minute. I'll meet you at the table."

After sitting with Ellie for a few minutes, I walked over to our table, so happy to see all my friends' smiling faces.

"Do my armpits smell?" I asked, moving close to Veronica.

Veronica sniffed in my direction and replied, "I don't smell you."

"I showered, I deodorized, and my shirt is clean, but I can still smell my pits."

Barbara said, "Honey, I keep telling you, your hormones are changing."

"Oh please, not the perimenopause thing again. You know, I've been getting in bad moods and smelling all my life. Not everything is hormone-related."

"She's a baby," Veronica said.

I hooked my arm inside Veronica's and patted her forearm. "My father used to say when I got in bad moods that I was tired. He would explain that just like a baby gets tired, so do adults. We just don't have someone to put us to bed when we cry."

I noticed Wolfgang walking around the restaurant. My father also would say, "Just because it does not last forever does not mean it wasn't good while it lasted." I imagine Barbara and Wolfgang had shared many wonderful times. They had a beautiful family and created an empire together. It just didn't last forever, and they were doing their best to get on with their lives.

Wolfgang stopped to say hello to us all—an awkward moment. I was new to the scene, but everyone else had seen Barbara through it all—babies being born, restaurants being built, parties, laughter, love, and family—and then the hurt and pain. They were a tight bunch who had each other's backs. When he leaned in to kiss everyone, some allowed it and others offered a hand. Barbara stood, arms folded, and said nothing.

After dessert, as the others took their leave, Barbara and I sat looking out onto the patio, where a few latecomers were still dining. A handsome man, a cross between Robert Redford and Steve Martin—walked by and smiled at Barbara. I sucked in a deep breath. "Oh, my God," I said. "That man looks so much like my father."

"I have to ask you something, Trish," Barbara said.

"Okay, let's have it." I cringe when people announce that they are going to ask you something, like you need a warning. Barbara was already the most brutally honest person I knew, so I braced myself.

"Have you ever considered contacting the man who killed your parents?"

"No way." The very idea freaked me out. I didn't even like to talk or think about him. "I wondered if he would contact one of us, but no, I have never considered contacting him."

As I reconsidered the question, I tried to stay open-minded. I thought about my sisters and what my parents would want. I had recently run a red light and if anyone should know the dangers of irresponsible driving, it should be me. I was driving Barbara's big Suburban and was not familiar with the weight of the car, so I blazed through the light, and the city of Beverly Hills sent a photo of me along with a $340 ticket to Barbara's house. She said the expression on my face was priceless. I apologized to Barbara and paid the ticket, of course. What else could I do to make it right?

It was too late for the man who killed my parents to help me with the pain. He had ten years to contact us," I said. "It would serve no purpose to talk to him now. Maybe it would relieve some of his guilt, if he has any, but his guilt is not my concern."

I suddenly felt raw and out of control. I just wanted to get in my car and drive until I couldn't drive any longer.

🌱 🌱 🌱

THE NEXT DAY, I stopped by Barbara's house after my morning carpool.

"I have hidden behind your love," I said. "And Terese's. Hoping you could take away the pain."

"Trish, I could never do that. I could never fill the void of your mother."

"I know, I know," I said, "and I'm fully aware that I have displaced emotions. But it's human emotion, and it's real emotion. It's what I do to survive—to cope. I found pieces of my mother in you and Terese; that made the pain bearable."

"Maybe that is what we are, pieces of your mother." She took my hand. "Trish, there are pieces of your mother inside of you too."

I looked down at Barbara's hand holding mine. I think this was my favorite of their shared similarities: their petite, delicate hands. I grew up so in love with my mother that I knew every aspect of her. She was covered in Irish freckles, and I could have drawn a map of them if I needed to. If you put one hundred different pairs of legs or hands (or any body part for that matter) in front of me, I could, without a doubt, pick out the pair that belonged to my mother. Her hands were my favorite, maybe because they were so delicate and reminded me of her vulnerability, or maybe because she held me with them so many times. They kept me safe, they touched my face, they rubbed my back, and they wiped my tears. I lifted Barbara's hand and held it with both of mine. Losing my mother was always my greatest fear in life. And here I was, surviving it.

Barbara cleared her throat and said, "Byron has informed me that he thinks he's getting a step-brother or -sister."

"Barbara, I'm sorry, this is so hard."

"Really, I'm okay, but Byron is upsetting me. Last night he was tossing a ball all around the house, kept hitting things."

"Take it easy on him," I said. "Sounds like it was a big day for everyone."

"Tricia, true, and I was patient for a while, but would you like it if Billy or Jack threw a ball and it hit your mother's art?" she asked in an angry tone.

"My mother's art is a little different than your collectibles."

"Sometimes you act like you are the only one who's ever been hurt, Tricia."

I shook my head, speechless.

"I'm just worried about my boys," she said. "I know today has to be difficult for them."

I tried to stay focused on her concerns; I could hear fear in her voice for her children. We continued talking for another few minutes, but I was having trouble pretending to be okay, so I fumbled around under my chair and got my purse.

"I'm sorry, Barbara, I need to go."

"Tricia, before you go," she said, "hear me: we are not always going to get along." She could tell I was upset.

"I understand that, but...I need to go."

"Okay," she said, and that was that. There was no "Love you," no "Talk to you tomorrow"—nothing.

At home, I sat and cried. What the hell had just happened? Barbara and I had never had words and now we had both hurt each other with them. My mind teemed with all the things I should have said, but I knew I should have said nothing. I should have done nothing but listen to her. She needed me. I didn't need to bring up my stuff at that time. It was her turn, and I did not let her have it. My head was so far up my ass, I was missing the pain of people I loved around me. Only Barbara, who I let in the closest, had the courage to speak the truth, and I trusted her enough to accept it as truth.

Have I hung on to it too long, am I being a victim, have I been present for others in their lives? I needed to take a good, hard look at myself.

❦ ❦ ❦

ON THE TENTH ANNIVERSARY of my parents' death, I set out to walk twenty miles—one mile to represent each year that had passed for each one of their deaths—but I made it only about twelve miles before stopping at Starbucks for a cup of tea to warm me. After another half a mile, I was overcome with such stomach pain I could not take another step. I bent over in front of the Federal Building on Wilshire Boulevard, cars whizzing by. I was dressed in sweats, looking pretty worn out with no money, no purse, nothing at all with me except my cell phone to call Liz and Eva. The combination of caffeine and excessive exercise was twisting my guts in a knot, but all the restaurants and stores on the block had bathrooms reserved for customers only. I did not look like a customer. I thought about homeless people and I thought about how cruel life can be to many.

Then I called home for a ride.

🌳 🌳 🌳

THE NEXT YEAR WAS GOOD, full of children healthily growing, loving friends, and family. It was two days before the eleventh anniversary of my parents' death. Up until a year ago, I would have said "the car accident." I was now able to say, "Their death."

I was walking out of the doctor's office with Jack and Bobby, heading to the car. Sitting in the front seat was a big deal in our family. It frustrated the boys that Olivia was allowed and they were not. Jack and Bobby had just completed their annual checkup. I told the boys that we could go anywhere they wanted, since they did such a great job getting their shots. We were going to Toys "R" Us.

"Will I be able to sit up front before Billy?" Jack asked.

"Billy's bigger than you, Jack," Bobby snapped.

I tried to diffuse the situation before it became a fight. "Jack, I think you will be big enough to sit in the front by the time you are in fifth or sixth grade."

"And then the airbag won't hurt me if it hits me?" he asked. "I wish I knew what it felt like. Too bad I can't ask your mom and dad."

"She doesn't have a mommy or daddy," Bobby protested.

"The airbags didn't go off in my mom and dad's car." I searched through my purse for the car keys. "They were stopped at a red light and another car hit them from behind."

"Oh, that's what happened," Jack said. "Wasn't the man driving eating KFC?"

"Yes, he was." I found the keys and hit the unlock button. "Get in."

"I bet it was McDonald's he was eating," Jack said. "You know McDonald's has greasy food and that can kill people."

"Honey, it wasn't the food that killed them. The man driving may have been looking down at his food and didn't see the light turn red. He didn't mean to hit their car. It was an accident."

Jack was still standing outside. Bobby crawled through the driver-seat door to the back of the car. "So, if he saw the light change colors, then your mom and dad would still be alive?" I motioned for him to get in the car, but he stood patiently waiting for an explanation.

"I don't know the answer to that, Jack. I'm not sure anymore if it is that simple. Please get in the car," I said firmly.

He climbed in and quickly buckled his seatbelt.

I asked, "So, what toy are you going to pick out?"

🌳 🌳 🌳

THE TEMPERATURE OF THE POOL water was tolerable. My feet cannot touch the bottom, so I move my legs and arms to stay afloat. I see Bobby swimming in front of me. He is doing well for just learning, but now he sinks under and struggles to reach the top. He panics and flails his body. His eyes widen. I try to reach out to him but I can't just won't move. Bobby is trying to reach me as he sinks lower. My legs move. I am able to swim closer to him. He is sinking under me. I can't move my arms. I can't help my baby; he is drowning. *Tricia, move your arms!* I swim down deeper and take his chin in my mouth. I bite down hard and pull him to the top of the water. My arms still dangle at my sides. My mouth still holds Bobby's chin as I drag him to the side. He grabs for the wall and pulls himself out to safety.

I wake up in a sweat. My head twirls trying to differentiate reality from my dream. My children are all alive and well. I saved my baby. They are safe. I fall back to sleep.

🌳 🌳 🌳

ON THE ELEVENTH ANNIVERSARY, I spent most of my day driving around, dropping the kids off at school, grocery shopping, picking up drycleaning, doing other motherly duties. By four o'clock in the afternoon, I still hadn't heard from Terese, which was unusual, so I emailed her a quick note to thank her for being part of my life and helping me through the pain.

Rich phoned as I was getting ready to leave the house. "Hi, how are you doing?"

"I'm good. I'm going to do my walk from 4:15 p.m. to 5:30 p.m.," I said. "Back east, the time would be 7:15 p.m. to 8:30 p.m." The hardest time for me. "Then Barbara asked me to come by."

"You do whatever you need to do. And Tricia, I love you."

"I love you too."

Olivia walked in the door minutes before I was ready to leave. "Hi, baby, how was school?"

"Good, are you going for your walk now?" she asked.

"Yes, and then I'll go to Barbara's. Are you okay with that?"

"Sure, Mom. I'll help Daddy; don't you worry about anything."

I walked over and gave her a big hug and kiss goodbye.

I was out the door at 4:10 p.m. so that by 4:15 p.m. I looked down at my watch and *bam*, 4:15 p.m.—that motherfucker slams into the back of my mother and father's car going at least sixty miles an hour, breaking both their necks. The impact sends their car spinning out into the intersection, glass smashing and flying everywhere. The back seat is now gone except for the small pocket of space where Juli-anne's tiny limp body rests, her unconscious head falling halfway out the side back window. Again, I ask, is it fate or luck?

Next: chaos. Strangers run to the car, call for help. The thoughts play over and over in my mind. As help arrives, they immediately go to Julianne. My parents were wearing their seatbelts, and all of their injuries were internal. They appeared okay. The officer said my father was slumped over onto my mother's shoulder, how beautifully perfect. Liz said Julianne's stomach had bruising on it from the seat-belt; however, my aunt said her friend was one of the ambulance attendants on call and that Julianne was put on the sidewalk and resuscitated. I don't know what really happened. We know they used the Jaws of Life to remove my father from the car. My mother was taken out through the car's passenger door. Strangers watched, one by one, as they slowly drove past, their evening plans delayed.

I wondered what they thought, caught in a traffic jam that stopped travel in both directions. I am sure there were some people who lowered their heads in prayer; others who may have thought how fortunate they were to be alive. Some may have driven by, quickly horrified by what they were witnessing; others may have slowed down as if they deserved a good look after waiting so long; and there may have been those excited by the intensity of the scene: "Wow, man, did you see that? That car was fucked up."

Yes, it was fucked up, very fucked up, and so were our lives as a result.

Of course, there were the heroes we will never know about and can never thank: the first people at the scene, those who used their cellphones to call for help, those who spoke quietly trying to reassure everyone in the car, maybe someone sang a lullaby to Julianne as they waited for help to arrive. We will never know. I think I can imagine, but maybe not, the sickness they felt in their stomachs, the fright as they waited helplessly. I do not think there was much blood. I don't think anyone in the car was conscious enough to moan. I wonder if, eleven years later, these people still think about that evening? I wonder what effect it may have had on their lives. Do they live differently? Do they appreciate the small things in life? Do they wonder if it could have been them, what if they were only one car ahead? Do they panic every time the light turns green? How sad the medical crew must have been when they went home to their own families that night. I bow to them now wherever they may be.

I walked and walked and found myself at St. Monica Church. In the grand cathedral adorned in stained glass and religious sculpture, I lit two candles and sat for a while on a hard wooden pew, but I did not pray. A young couple was practicing for their upcoming wedding. I watched, enjoying their excitement, and then headed over to Barbara's house.

"Are you okay?" she asked.

"I feel good." I nodded. "I think I may even feel good about feeling good."

"Great. You have a massage in ten minutes, so go get ready," she said.

When the massage was through, I lay on the bed and rested, feeling relaxed for the first time in a long time. I'd never seen Barbara like this—dressed in gray sweatpants and T-shirt, hair pulled back, no jewels, no makeup. She looked beautiful.

"How was your massage?"

"Wonderful," I said. "Thank you again."

We didn't get into any heavy conversation. We just lay there and rested our tired souls and minds. I felt so safe and loved. It amazed me to think we had known each other for only a couple of years. She felt like family, someone I had known all my life. I thought again, is it all chance or is it meant to be? She was so different from anyone my mother had ever known, yet could my mother have sent her? We sat quietly for a while, both lost in our own thoughts.

I wondered if my father had seen the car coming up on them in his rearview mirror. I remembered how relieved my sisters and I were when the police officer stated in court that the driver never hit the brakes. There were no skid marks, which means there were no horrible sounds for them to hear before impact. But what about the car accelerating, did they hear that? And what about the car he sideswiped before hitting them? Did they hear that and turn their heads before they were crushed themselves? Was there terror before impact? Did my mother scream out?

Barbara broke our silence. "I'm so sorry," she said, looking straight through my soul. My eyes immediately welled up with tears, but I held her gaze and did not look away. I searched her face for answers I knew she did not have. I looked past her to the stained glass window. My mind smashed through it with my foot. Barbara's eyes remained calm, holding me safe, as my mind spiraled into my own personal hell. I felt naked, exposed. Anxiety overwhelmed me, and in my mind, I went back to the window, heaving my whole body into the magnificent blues and purples, oranges and greens. I curled into a fetal position and imagined myself spinning, letting the glass penetrate every inch of my skin. And then I plunged my chest directly on top of the shattered glass, feeling it pierce directly through my heart. There was blood, lots of blood. My anger became violent. I didn't want to go there tonight. I didn't want to hurt, to confront.

Barbara held me like a prisoner in her calm, gentle gaze, peaceful, honest. The love, the trust, it was too much for me to bear.

"Tricia, you're safe. Let go, baby."

She touched my face, delicately wiping the tears that flowed from my eyes. There was nowhere to hide. Barbara's eyes became a looking glass. I could see myself, eleven years earlier, in the hospital room with my mother. White room, white sheets, my mother's hospital gown was white, her body silent, her eyes closed. Soft brown hair framed her pale, beautiful face so perfectly. She must have curled it, I thought, before leaving the house with my father and Julianne.

offered me comfort. These were my final minutes with her. We'd been told that she was gone from us now and forever. I was curled in her arms like a child, resting comfortably. I draped her arm around me and played with her hands, touching each fragile finger one by one. Her skin seemed paper thin, and her knuckles were bony, but she was warm to the touch. I put her hand to my face and let her feel the dampness of my tears.

"Please, don't be sad. You're safe now," I heard my mother say.

I don't know now, nor did I know then, if it was Barbara who spoke. I only know I heard my mother's voice. I stayed there for a while, trying so hard not to let her go as moments passed, maybe minutes, maybe hours. Since the night of the accident, the days and years that followed, I had never once cried in anyone's arms like that, including Rich's, and God knows he tried. The last person I let hold me while I cried was my mother in her hospital bed—her deathbed.

❦ ❦ ❦

AS I DROVE HOME LATER, I felt a force of loving-kindness that I'd never felt before. The house was dark, and as I headed up the stairs to bed I remembered a promise I had made to Terese. She had emailed me back earlier, before I set out: "I bet you'll be able to see your mother and father tonight in the stars. Promise to look? I'll be looking for you looking for them."

I turned and headed back down the stairs and out the front door. The Santa Monica air was warm and moist, embracing my skin. I walked barefoot into my flower garden. Some purple flowers stood tall, proud they had survived until September. A slow drizzle of water flowing from the mouth of our fountain could be heard over the faint sounds of insects. I sat, and the bench was cold: goose bumps covered my skin from head to toe. The discomfort reminded me I was alive, living this moment.

I was scared, actually petrified, but I dropped to my knees and rested my arms upon the ceramic bench in front of me. I knew the sky was crystal clear, and I could tell by the shadow of my silhouette that the moon had to be about somewhat full. I resisted looking up and watched an ant carry her horde across the cool white bench. A tear dropped down in front of her. She simply walked around it. I could go back inside now and everything would be the same in the morning. The life I had learned to live with would be undisturbed. I feared disturbing it. I feared saying goodbye to it. Who would I be without it? Would I lose them if I lost the pain? The tears turned to sobs as I searched myself for courage, murmuring, "Everyone is waiting. Trust in the love, Tricia. Trust in the love."

Cautiously, I tilted my head to the sky and witnessed the beauty of the night. What appeared to be hundreds, maybe thousands, of stars were dancing in the sky, some only a small flicker while others dazzled. The moon, three-fourths full, was bright yet distant as it made its journey across the world.

I searched the galaxy for the two stars that held their souls. Were they laughing? Were they crying? Were they waiting? Did they know I was here?

I could taste blood as I bit down on my lip. I continued to study the stars until I found them: they were sitting side by side straight on top of my home, watching over us as we slept. The light they cast was almost chilling. It was my parents. I knew it. It suddenly felt easier to do what I had to do. I took a deep breath and exhaled. Then, for the first time in eleven years, I spoke in a voice I faintly remembered, "Dear Mom and Dad, guess what? I have four babies..."

🌳 🌳 🌳

ONE NIGHT, AS I LAY with Jack in the darkness of his room, rubbing his back and going over the day's events, we heard a faint noise. I presumed it came from the front window as someone passed by. Jack presumed differently. "Mom, did you hear that? It was your mother. Sometimes she comes to say goodnight to me," he said with the clarity of pure innocence.

Tears welled up in my eyes. The realization that he believed my mother was coming to him to say goodnight, that he had created a relationship with her that I was unaware of and incapable of doing myself, was so painful yet beautiful.

We lay silent for a few moments and then Jack spoke again. "Mom, do you know what I don't get?"

"What?" I asked carefully, not knowing what he was possibly going to say next.

"The island of Kauai is so peaceful, so why do they use it to film such violent movies?"

This first-grader was getting a little too intense for me. "Not sure, babe, but you really should get to sleep now." I leaned over and kissed his forehead and headed downstairs to sit with Rich.

🌱 🌱 🌱

THE FOLLOWING SEPTEMBER rolled around, and I was in a good place. The kids were flourishing and had great friends. Rich and I were having fun and getting out with other couples. Barbara and the other girls became family. Life felt full, and I was not dreading the month as I had so many times before.

"Enough about me," I told Barbara. "It's about you now."

She and Wolfgang were closing one of the restaurants they'd built in Malibu during the best days of her family life. I knew it was painful for her, so I decided to turn around this month that had pulverized me for eleven years and make it all about someone else.

I told her, "I promise to be a good friend and only listen the whole month of September." I made a commitment to wish her something good every night. The first night I sent her this email: "Dear Barbara, today, September 1, 2005, I wish you, Trust."

I continued writing a simple wish every night or sometimes in the morning if I could get to the computer. And then the phone rang. It rang just like it had almost twelve years to the day earlier. Again, my sister's voice. "Tricia. Tricia. You need to come home."

This time it was Aaron, gone at twenty. An overdose.

I ran to the bathroom and shoved a towel in my mouth so the children would not hear my animal-sounding wails. Every cell in my body screamed out, my legs went limp, and I fell to the floor, holding my head trying to stop my thoughts. One of the children yelled out, so I struggled to the outside of the house and sobbed. An hour later I had packed my bags and I went down the stairs, where Vanessa, Dorothy, Sheila, and Mary Jane were waiting for me. Dorothy assured me she would help with the children. Rich would stay with the kids and follow in a couple of days. Sheila offered to take the flight with me, but I felt okay to handle it alone. The kids were all sleeping, and I did not want them to see me so upset—Rich would have to tell them. I called Terese as Mary Jane drove me to the airport. I had already called Barbara, who was in New York. She would take the train into Trenton the next day.

I knew the drill and the horrific hell ahead of us.

The week was a blur. Just as we had begun to trust life again, to stop waiting for the next tragedy to hit, tragedy hits. I had now lost my parents in a car accident and my nephew to a drug overdose. But my sister had lost her parents and now her son. Walking into her bedroom the night I flew in and finding her lying on her bed just hours after she'd lain in bed holding her deceased child was the most sickening moment of my life—a hell few will know in life. And the world expects me to believe everything happens for a reason? We are given only what we can handle. How and why does one family have so much suffering and loss?

Liz asked me if I was okay burying my parents' ashes, which had been sitting on her living room mantelpiece the past twelve years, with Aaron's at the local cemetery. Of course. Whatever she needed. We buried Aaron and our mother and father together on September 16, 2005, exactly twelve years to the day after my parents were killed.

Driving out of the cemetery that morning, I blurted to Liz from the back seat of the car, "We should have made sure Mommy was in the middle, between Daddy and Aaron."

Since my parents shared an urn, I knew one of them had to be placed in the middle.

"I did."

🌿 🌿 🌿

RETURNING TO LOS ANGELES after the funeral, I needed my friends more than ever; our circle of love grew closer. Sheila and I got our kids together more often. Dorothy came over to the house a lot. Keeping my promise to Barbara, I never stopped writing the wishes, finding comfort in anything consistent.

And then Rich informed me of the opportunity he had back east. We would be moving, again.

I knew this drill too. Everyone would mean well and swear that nothing would change. However, lives would get busy and eventually everyone would become a holiday card with a couple of phone calls in between. The thought of losing Barbara, of our friendship's fading away with time and space, made my heart ache. She assured me she was different, that her home would always be mine to come home to, and I knew she believed that.

But she had not moved in thirty years, and this would be my fourth move in twelve.

We did the same drill as we had done before. Rich moved to start his new job, and I stayed back until the kids finished out the school year. Then summer came and we said our goodbyes.

As I boarded that plane from Los Angeles, heading to our next home in Connecticut, I had a story to tell about human kindness and how it can save our lives with love and trust by filling the voids that choke us. But there was a lot I didn't know.

I did not know which friend sounded more absurd to me in her parting comments: Leeza asking me if I was lonely, or Sheila, suggesting that I would become the most spiritual of us all.

Lonely? What did that even mean? I had Rich and the kids. I was always surrounded by family and friends. I had never been lonely in my life.

Spiritual? Everyone close to me knew I'd fought for a relationship with God, but it had never happened. I'd thought the bright side of my tragedy would be that it could open me up to God, but it didn't, and I'd given up on finding it.

I didn't know that loneliness is one of the cruelest emotions one can experience. I did not know a relationship with God could be found in silence and reflection.

"And I didn't know you, Martha."

PART FOUR

ALONE, TOGETHER

I came to see that I just needed to learn to be alone without feeling lonely.

CHAPTER 10

I'll Just Tell Martha

"Martha, what is a life without trust but a life of fear? And there is no peace in a life of fear. So yes, it looks like I have it all, but I can't appreciate the good stuff when my head is so far up my ass with the bad stuff. But tell me this, Martha. Let's say you walk into a room and out of nowhere, you get hit in the face—*bam! bam!*—twice. You get hit so hard, your face is all bashed up, and it takes forever to recover. So then every time you walk into that room, you put your hands up to protect yourself from getting hurt again. But then, Martha, you finally begin to trust again, you put your hands at your side, and *bam!* Fucking *bam!*"

With September nearing, I felt myself becoming anxious. The month brought with it the day my parents were killed, and now we had the anniversary of Aaron's death too. The anticipation of the week was difficult. It was one thing to feel the loss, but in September my mind wanted to brood on the actual day of death. I was flooded with the terrible memories of Liz's voice, "You need to come home," of crying with her on the bed, holding my nieces and nephew while they cried, of witnessing the misery of everyone who loved Aaron, of seeing his family sitting behind his coffin and then lowering what remained of this child into the ground. Every fucking horrible memory pushed its way to the front of my mind to torture me.

And once that was over, the week would drag on as I anticipated the punishment of my mother's and my father's death. My father's swollen face, lying with my mother and then leaving her to die alone. Why, why did I leave her alone? Why, Tricia, why? And I was unable to deny the sad reality that if my parents had not been killed, then Aaron might have lived. The sun rose and set with Aaron in my parents' eyes: he was the first grandchild and a boy, yet. My father called him every day, and every Friday night he slept at their house. Aaron was extremely close to my mother. When they died, a piece of Aaron died too.

Our first Christmas after the accident, my sisters and I bought each other and the kids lots of gifts, like my mother would have done for everyone. We sat in Liz's living room, but Aaron would not come downstairs. He was a nine-year-old boy who was too heartbroken to open presents. He just lay on his bottom bunk staring at the mattress springs above him. He was never the same after my parents died. He never trusted life again and did what he had to do to numb the pain. It was the trickle-down effect of the suffering caused by that car accident.

I was afraid to show anyone the raw anguish living inside of me, fearing they would run. I could no longer look to Liz for support, because her plight was unthinkable. It was my job now to be her support. My friends and family had been there enough. September was not their burden to bear, and I had already dragged them through it all plenty.

I decided I would go about my life and let the month come and go, do the motions without the emotions. But no matter how loud I played the music in the car or on my iPod while walking, the voices in my head screamed louder. Past Septembers, I could shove some of the pain deep away, but with all my walks and all my time alone, I was exposed, raw:

There is a sickness in the stomach, a hole so vast that only the hole in the heart can contend with it. A strange silence echoes the air, yet people are talking, their mouths are moving. I scream but no one hears me. I need to stop the madness, yet I do not know how.

🌳 🌳 🌳

SEPTEMBER 11 ARRIVED; the country mourned the anniversary of the World Trade Center attack and our family mourned the death of a child. I reached out to Liz and her family and then spent the day doing the usual routine. Ugly, uncomfortable thoughts came into my mind. I allowed them their time and then sent them on their way.

The following evening, Olivia needed a ride home from a friend's house. I picked her up and asked her about her evening. We came up on a red light, so I stopped and continued talking, now able to look at her. I glanced in my rearview mirror and could see an SUV coming towards us with no signs of stopping. I yelled out to Olivia, 'We are going to get hit!'"

And *bam!* We got hit. I was able to pull the car over to the side of the road, but I was so shaken I could not get out. I had always wondered if my father had seen the car coming; did he yell out? Now it had happened to me. I actually experienced the emotion that I would never know if he had. The moment was over almost before I could finish crying out.

I called the police; the woman who had hit us came up to our car and it was obvious that she had been drinking. The police took her away with her hands cuffed behind her back, leaving her teenaged daughter sitting in the front seat and a toddler sitting in a car seat waiting for a relative to come pick them up.

It was frightening in one breath and heartbreaking in another.

The next day I tried to shake it off. Olivia ended up getting a major headache, but was physically fine. I remembered when I had asked Terese if I would always be the girl whose parents had been killed in a car accident and she had said, if I wanted to be. No, that was not who I wanted to be or who I needed to be. I didn't want to win the tragedy contest, or be spoken about with pity any more.

I will not allow myself to wallow in a long storm of bitterness or self-pity, so I let the pain blow in and out like an afternoon thunderstorm clearing the air.

🌳 🌳 🌳

SEPTEMBER MARCHED ON. I walked, thinking about the accident. I cried thinking about my mother. I cried thinking about my father. And I felt sick thinking about Aaron. I allowed myself to think about thoughts I had not before. I questioned what my mother would say to me if she were given five minutes to return.

I love you more than you ever will know. Be strong, you can do this; I will always be with you.

And my father.

Never forget how good you are. Live your life with joy. Take care of Rich.

Then I thought about the maternal love Terese and Barbara had given me, and instead of shoving it back in my head, I sat with Martha and cried it out. It is time to let it hurt, feel it, scream at it, cry with it.

Release your anger and melt away your pain with love and acceptance. Be safe to trust. Your pain is real, but so are peace and happiness, and they have been patiently waiting for you right inside the gates of your emotions. I wish for you the release of your pain and anger.

"Martha, I am so tired of being sad. I don't want to be sad anymore." I took my sweater off and laid it on the grass and then lay down in front of Martha. "Do you want to hear about it, Martha, the night my parents died?"

So I began.

🌳 🌳 🌳

IT WAS A TYPICAL Thursday night. My mother knew I was trying to teach Olivia to sleep through the night. She knew it was hard on me to let her cry. We decided she would come up the next day and spend the night with us. It was a Jewish holiday and she would be off from work. My mom said she would call. "Okay, honey, I'll talk to you in a few hours. Enjoy your class. I love you" were the last words I'd hear her speak.

When the phone rang that night, I thought it was her calling, but it wasn't. It was my sister Liz telling me there had been an accident. Someone from St. Mary's Hospital called her saying a young girl gave them this number. They told her the child was conscious and okay, but they didn't say much more about our parents except they were brought to two different hospitals. Liz said she would call me back when she knew more. I called the emergency room at the hospital where my father had been taken and spoke to his nurse. She suggested I come home.

Carol came with me. On the train I decided: I could handle whatever they needed. No matter how hurt they were, I would move home and take care of them. We were all going to be fine.

When we got off the train, I was greeted at the station by a few of my closest high school friends, Lisa, Mary Jo, and Jill. They had grown up with me, and they loved my parents very much. This was not a good sign they were all there. Then my sister called my cellphone and told me to go directly to my father's hospital—she was already at my mother's, because this was where her daughter, Julianne, had been admitted after the accident. Julianne had a broken ankle and a concussion. In what seemed to be the longest drive of my life, we rode to Stone Valley Hospital in silence.

"What the fuck," I said as we pulled into the parking lot. There, standing in the entrance to the emergency room, were over a dozen friends and relatives. The men had their hands in their pockets and their heads down "What's everyone doing here?" I asked. Then I got out of the car and walked right past everyone. No one tried to stop me. I entered the ER, and my sister Eva came running towards me, hysterical. "We are going to lose them both," she said. "Liz says we are going to lose them both." Our sister Liz was in her third year of training to become a physician's assistant.

I brushed Eva aside. A nurse walked over and ushered me to the back. Then a very young-looking doctor approached me. There was no one else standing in the hall. The nurse walked away, giving us privacy. The walls were yellow. We were in front of a set of double doors, but I didn't know where they led.

"Hi, I'm Dr. Hanes. I first want to tell you that your father did nothing wrong. He was not at fault. His car was hit by another car."

This information seemed pointless.

He continued, "I'm sorry to tell you, but the injuries your father withstood were life-changing. If he lives, he will never be the same."

I was no longer in my own body. I was looking down watching a nightmare unfold.

"Your father's injuries have left him paralyzed, and his brain is showing no activity."

"Look, I don't mean to offend you," I said. "But you seem very young. I would like to speak to someone else."

"Okay," he said, and exhaled. "I'll get the head of the department for you."

"And I want him helicoptered to Philadelphia, now!" I demanded.

He turned back to me and reached out his hand. I stepped back, avoiding his contact. "Philadelphia cannot help him. There are no brain signals. Your father will never be the same...."

Never the same, never the same, never the same....

"...would you like to see him?"

"No! I want to speak to the department head."

He nodded and walked me over to a phone. After a few 'okay, okays' he handed the phone to me. A kind but serious voice on the other line confirmed that my father was brain-dead. The young doctor gently touched my arm and held out his other, signaling the direction to my father. I walked down a short hall to the back of the ER, an area meant to give us as much privacy as possible. I pulled the curtain open and every cell in my body went numb. There lay my once powerful, muscular father limp on a gurney. The man who had protected me and had provided for me my whole life, now lay before me lifeless. A white sheet covered him from the neck down. His once handsome face was swollen, and there were drops of blood near his nose and mouth, but it was his neck that stood out the most. It was swollen almost to the size of his head.

I walked to the foot of his gurney and bent down over him. Blood had filled his eardrums. I placed my trembling hands on the sides of his head and whispered, "Daddy, I'm here. I need you to fight now. . Come on. You can do it! Please, Daddy, fight real hard." I put my lips on his forehead. He felt clammy and cool. "Please, Daddy, I love you! Please, Daddy, wake up. Wake up."

I wanted to run, but I could barely move my legs.

I stayed with him only for a short time. I could not bear it one more moment. I staggered down the stark hospital hallway towards my friends. A couple of them walked towards me, but I kept going. I was rambling about calling Rich. I felt as physically weak as if I had just given birth and was now trying to walk. I was gone in my own world.

I called my apartment, and a neighbor answered. He said Rich was already on his way. I phoned Rich's sister, Dorothy. All I could say was, "There has been an accident. My father may die, and I don't know if my mother is going to die too."

The hospital moved my friends and I into a small private room. There was a square table that we all sat around as we waited for word of any changes. Then there was a knock on the door. A skinny little man with a kind face stepped inside.

"Hello," he said as he reached for my hand. "I'm here from the Organ Donation and Transplant Association of America."

"Excuse me?" I said in disbelief. "You have to be kidding me." I turned to my friends. "This is crazy. Why is he here?"

No one spoke. My friends hung their heads in silence.

"I'm not interested; there is no way I'm signing anything." I thought, *If I sign away his parts, they'll stop trying to help him. It's all happening so fast, I can't think.*

He placed the papers down and excused himself. I shoved them off the table to the floor and cried and cried and cried. Everyone cried. Doctors would come every so often and report that nothing had changed. The man from the donors' organization sat alone outside in the hall. I don't know who I hated more: him or the young doctor who delivered the news.

I called Liz.

"Trishy." She called me a name from our childhood. "Trishy, it's what Daddy would want. I think you need to sign the papers."

Oh my God, what is happening? Make it stop! Please, stop! Stop!

I hung up the phone and picked up the pen.

Mary Jo had left the hospital earlier to go get Rich and Olivia. She would take the baby home with her after dropping Rich off. It must have been two o'clock in the morning when

I heard Rich come running down the hospital hall crying, "Oh, baby, oh my God."

About an hour later, Liz called. "Tricia, they are going to move Mommy to a room. She is stable."

"Stable, does that mean she is going to be okay?"

"She is stable right now. You should come see her."

I yelled to everyone: "My mother is stabilized! She is going to be okay. I'll take care of her." I'll take care of her. She can live with us, and I'm sure my sisters want her to live with them too. We will all take care of her and make her better. It will be okay. I'll hold her and let her cry about Daddy forever if she needs to. I'll make her better. No more bad things will happen. "Rich, she can live with us, right?"

Rich came up behind me and placed his hand on my back. "Of course. But Tricia, we should go to St. Mary's now and see her."

I was frightened by this. "No, Rich, Liz is there with her. She said she is okay. I should go be with Olivia. I can go later to see my mother."

"Tricia, I really think we should go," he repeated.

I reluctantly gave in, but I asked to see my father again first. Rich came with me. Hours had passed, and my father continued to look like someone I did not know. Again, I walked to his head and spoke to him, but I could not touch him this time. I whispered, "Daddy, I have to go check on Mommy now. I'll be back real soon." My tears fell onto his face, and I was too scared to wipe them away.

Rich stood behind me with his hands on my shoulders.

"Daddy, I'm sorry I signed the papers. I didn't want to do it. It means nothing. Please, Daddy, keep fighting. You can do it. Keep fighting."

When Rich and I left, it was around 3:00 a.m. It was so weird because inside the hospital it was so bright, and the lights outside were real bright, but it was so late at night.

My friend Sally drove us over to St. Mary's hospital, where my mother and Julianne had been taken. It was rainy and gray. Fog made it difficult to see far in the distance. We drove for about twenty minutes and then, out of nowhere, the hospital appeared: big, white, up on a hill. My sister Liz was waiting for us at the front door and led us to ICU.

We walked quietly down the long halls and rode up the elevators in silence, until we finally reached my mother's unit. There were no rooms on the floor, just beds surrounded by white curtains to give the patients privacy. My mother's bed was located directly across from the nurses' station. Her curtain was closed. Liz had said earlier that they were moving her to a private room...I stopped and stood still in the hall.

Liz walked forward and opened the curtain. Rich and Sally stood behind me. I slowly walked over to my mother's bed. She looked good—peaceful—and she seemed comfortable, wrapped up in white cotton hospital sheets. I bent over and kissed her on the cheek. She was warm and soft. I stroked her hair and told her all about my father. I lied and told her he would be okay.

There was nowhere to sit, and sick people were everywhere. There were sounds of phones ringing and machines beeping. Everything was so surreal; I was in a trance. I told her we had to go check on Olivia, but that I would be back soon.

We walked out into the parking lot. I couldn't see far because it was so foggy and dark, but I could hear someone walking across the gravel. Then, in the dark mist, appeared a man. He was walking towards us. Still I couldn't make him out; the thick fog shaded his face. Finally, he came into sight: the man from the organ donors' association.

I asked, "What are you doing here?"

He just looked down at the ground in front of him.

"Please don't tell me you came for my mother." I turned to Rich. "Tell him she's stabilized and to go home. My mother is okay. We don't need you here. Leave us alone."

He reached out and touched my shoulder. "I'm sorry, but the hospital called me."

He slowly walked past us to the entrance of the hospital door.

I dropped to all fours and began to vomit. I heaved until my body broke. A part of me died, right then and there. I desperately wanted my mother to hold me, and how desperately I wanted my father to tell me I was going to be okay.

We got to Mary Jo's house after 4:00 a.m. Olivia was peacefully sleeping, so Rich insisted I lie down. Four hours later, Rich and I drove to my father's hospital. It was so difficult being with him, because his hospital didn't go to the same extreme to make him appear comfortable. He still lay in the back room of the ER on the gurney; his face was even more swollen. He no longer looked like my father. I think I kissed him goodbye, but really, I can't remember. It definitely wasn't a final goodbye, just an "I need to go see Mom" goodbye.

Eva went to see my father after I left, and while she was there, his body began to shut down. She was alone with him when blood began to ooze from his eyes, nose, and ears. They pronounced him dead at 8:30 that morning, but none of us were with him. He would be okay with that. In fact, he would have insisted that we all go to be with our mother.

When I got to my mom's hospital, she had been moved to her own room. She was in a nice bed and they kept a heating pad on her so she was warm, not like my father. He was cold. My mom looked like she was sleeping. She was covered with the blankets but her arms were stretched out lying alongside of her. Her hair looked brushed. The nurses were so nice to us. All of my mother's brothers were there. She had four of them, but her sister was out of town and on an airplane trying to get back to us. Lots of cousins were there also. I lay with her and I would open her eyelids and look into her eyes. I kissed her face again and again and told her who was coming in and out of her room. I remember the sound of crying and 'Oh, my God' as people walked in and out. We got the call that my father was pronounced dead, but I can't tell you where I was or who told me. Can you imagine that? I can't tell you who told me my father was dead.

Anyway, I do remember climbing onto the bed with my mother and stroking her arm. Then I took her hand and cupped it around my face. It felt so nice against my skin. I kept it there for a minute pretending she was holding me. I upset the others in the room; their moans and weeping became louder. My mother's sister, Marie, finally arrived around 3:00 p.m. She was surrounded by her eight children and rushed to my mother's side. They were very close, the only girls born to a family of six Irish Catholics growing up in a coal miners' town in Pennsylvania. My aunt sobbed as she looked down at her little sister, the one woman who had been by her side her entire life. I was in a daze as I watched my aunt. It was like being hung and whipped; eventually you can't make out one lashing from another.

The doctor called me and my sisters into a conference room to discuss my mother's condition.

"We would like to do one last scan to see if there is any activity in your mother's brain, if that's okay?"

We sat speechless. He continued, "If we don't find any activity, we will unplug the ventilator and let her breathe on her own."

We sat in the hall and waited. We paced. We would sit next to a relative who would try to comfort us. I remember sitting and watching Rich walk up and down the hall crying. He was lost. The test came back and again they asked Eva, Liz, and me to go into the little room. This time a pastor was there and the hospital social worker. The doctor simply said, "I'm very sorry."

I stood up and made my way to my mother's room. The nurses were with her, but left as I entered. I climbed up on the bed with her and lay down, resting my head on her stomach. I picked up her arm and studied the pattern of her freckles that I knew so well, and then I draped it over me. I remember smelling her too. I think, for the last moment in my life, I felt safe. It was the only time I had been totally alone with her, and I was comfortable being with her. I lay on the bed curled up with her arms wrapped around me. I looked over at the clock and realized it was 4:30 p.m. Exactly twenty-four hours ago I had talked to my mother about her coming to visit me the next day. We had spent the day together, but it wasn't what we had in mind. I thought about how ironic it was that I lay with her, curled up resting on her stomach as she died and that this was also how I started my life with her, curled in her arms in a hospital bed.

Time passed, not much, but a nurse came in to get me. I wish now they had let me stay there until I made the decision to go myself. I wish now we would have stayed once they unplugged the machines, but we had been through enough. Eva and Liz said their goodbyes. We were all standing in the hall when a nurse signaled to Liz that Julianne was ready to go home. We all walked down the hall towards the children's ward. Julianne sat in a wheelchair waiting at the end of the hall. She had no idea what was happening, but she must have been scared to see so many people. I don't remember anyone crying at this point but I'm sure we all were...or maybe not. Liz pushed her wheelchair out in front, as we all fell behind. We walked out of the hospital, beaten, defeated, broken.

"So that's my story, Martha. Those are the memories I try to suppress as I lie awake in bed at night. You okay, Martha? Are you okay? Do you want me to continue, or are you so depressed, you are going to turn brown?"

The night my parents died, my sisters and I were never once in the room together. If one of us was next to my mother or father, the others would go out to the hallway with friends and relatives. We all had our own posse seated at our sides, protecting us from any unwanted intrusion. The day of the service, we all arrived in separate cars and sat in three different pews. I hugged every person who traveled near and far to pay their respects on that day, but there was no way in the world I could bear to wrap my arms around my sisters. I lost eleven pounds in four days between the accident and the funeral. My body and mind were shut down. Acknowledging my sisters' pain was simply impossible. And at no time did either of them try to console me.

The saddest moments of my life took place weeks after my parents' death. My oldest sister, Eva, came to stay with me for a few days in New York. We walked the streets of Manhattan and played games with Olivia. At night, we watched movies, desperately trying to escape our reality, if just for a moment. After an exhausting day of meaningless acts of denial, I looked down at my sister and there she sat on my wooden floor, legs crossed with a glass of vodka in her hands, her head hung low. She just sat there and wept. Her hair was draped across her face and her body was slumped. Frozen in my own grief, I sat and watched her. I watched as her whimpers turned to sobs. I could not bear to see her in such pain. I felt shameful and pathetic for not reaching out and holding her, but I could not move.

It was surreal being at their home in the days following their death, searching through their drawers, my mother's purse, and my father's wallet. I took a photo of my mother lying on the beach from my father's wallet. She was young and full of life. It seemed so wrong, such a tremendous invasion of privacy, to have two people alive one minute and then to search through their stuff the next. I remember smelling every piece of clothing I touched, noticing the dishes in the sink, and finding the Christmas presents my mother had already purchased for us. I found a repair slip for my father's shoe and immediately drove over to the store. The Closed sign was up, and they waved me away, but I went crazy on them, banging on the window yelling, "Open this door; I want my father's shoes now!"

I'm surprised they opened up and didn't call the police. They handed me the shoes in a brown paper bag with a note from the repairman that read, "Sorry, too damaged to repair." I hugged the bag to my chest and stumbled back out into the cold. That was so my father. He would never kill an insect or throw away a favorite pair of shoes.

Weeks later I returned to sign some papers. I drove through my hometown as I had so many times before. It was quiet and the sky was miserable. The pond was frozen, and there was no sign of the mallards that lived there most of the year. The few people walking the street moved quickly with their heads down. Snow covered the rooftops of old buildings lining the square. I turned my mother's car onto Afton Avenue heading towards the Stone River. I didn't want to go in this direction, but something deep inside me took over. I tortured myself with a mind game: it was just another day that I was driving along the Stone River to their home, so familiar, so comforting, so taken for granted. I could see the house from a distance through the bare winter trees, a lovely English Tudor with a magnificent slate roof, stained glass windows, and arched doorways. My family's life took place in this home. Babies were born, weddings were celebrated, and teenagers came of age. We loved here, fought here. We lived here. My mother believed there were ghosts on the property, but I teased her that she was losing her mind.

I didn't see any cars in the snow-covered driveway, so I pulled in and drove around to the back, where I always parked my car. I looked up to the window of my mother's bedroom where we used to lie on her bed and talk. The new occupants had removed the priceless Japanese maple from the front yard. The romantic curtains were gone from the living room windows, the urns from the front steps. Looking out into the yard, I pictured my mother standing in the garden. My father sat in his favorite lounge chair reading the local newspaper, *The Trentonian*. It felt so real, so good. There was my mother coming through the kitchen door, calling, "Drive carefully, baby!" She looked beautiful. I loved it when she curled her hair and wore her gold hoop earrings.

Banging my fist on the steering wheel, I screamed so long and so hard, I could taste blood running down the back of my throat. I screamed until I was exhausted, so filled with emotion I wanted to crawl out of my skin. I closed my eyes and pictured the back door, pictured myself smashing it, smashing the windows that lined the back of the house. One by one, I drove my foot straight through them, leaving shattered glass everywhere. The bedroom windows—*smash! Smash! Smash!* This time I used my fist. I smashed every window in the house. Then I wiped my face, drove my mother's car back to my sister's place, took a cab to the train station, and headed home to Manhattan, where I ordered dinner and read Olivia a goodnight story before nursing her to sleep.

🌱 🌱 🌱

"So there it is, Martha. That is my story." I closed my eyes and tried to think happy thoughts, to recall a time when I felt whole.

I'm thirty years old and have been a mother for exactly forty-eight hours. The most beautiful creature I have ever laid eyes on lies curled up nuzzled in the warmth of my body. I press her close to my chest, hoping the familiar rhythm of my heartbeat will offer her comfort. My mother rests next to me. Rich walks in the room but does not disturb the silence. He leans over and kisses my head. As he walks back towards the door, I look to my mother. She has tears in her eyes. As always, her tears move me and I let the emotion flow from within me.

This is the best moment I had ever known in my life.

🌱 🌱 🌱

Time moved on in Connecticut, and Rich was approached by a head-hunter. He was happy with his current position and company, so usually would not pay much attention to the call; however, this one call got his attention. No so much the job but the location. "I got a call today from a headhunter about a job in Los Angeles."

My heart skipped a beat. "Are you interested?" I asked.

"I am interested in having a happy wife."

I remained quiet, not knowing what to say. We had been in Connecticut for over a year, and things just seemed worse; but I thought I was hiding it well. The kids were settled, but they still had a foot in LA, so moving back would be easy for them. Leaving Liz would be difficult, but I also knew how much she loved me in LA so she had a warm place to visit. Oh my God, was it possible that I might find myself back in Los Angeles?

I walked that night and then sat with Martha.

"Martha, we might move back to Los Angeles. Don't worry, I will call you from there. Weird thing is, Martha, it doesn't feel right. It's all I wanted, and now that it is a possibility, it doesn't seem right. Look at you. You can't run away every time things get tough. I wonder if you wish you could on bitter cold winter nights. No, Martha, I can't run. I have to beat this before I can move on from it. If we were to leave now, I would feel like I failed myself. Like you, I must face what life is handing me and see it through."

I smiled at Martha and headed into the house. "Goodnight, Miss Martha, I love you."

That night, while lying in bed, I said to Rich, "I don't think you should interview for that job. Your current job is right for you, and the kids are just settling in."

"Tricia?"

"What?"

"Nothing. Goodnight."

And that was the end of it.

I was determined to overcome my loneliness, this sorrow. I had been through too much to let life beat me now, and my family needed me whole. I did not want to be sad and mourning all of my life. I wanted to be happy. Barbara wanted me to go to therapy, but I had no interest. I believed in therapy, but I was not depressed. I was sad for a good reason. Talking about it wasn't going to change it. I was going to change it. I was not one to stay in bed or hit the bottle in the afternoon—I was more the type to take action. I went to different churches, but never found one that I clicked with. So I continued to walk the many beautiful trails the town had to offer with a different attitude. I noticed certain trees that were beautiful, and named them after people I loved. I smelled the air and felt the ground. I spent a lot of time with my thoughts. I needed time, a lot of time.

Then, I came across a book while shopping, *Change Your Thoughts—Change Your Life: Living the Wisdom of the Tao*, by Wayne Dyer. I opened it on impulse and read, "I know that we humans are like the rest of the natural world and that sadness, fear, frustration or any troubling feeling cannot last. Nature doesn't create a storm that never ends. Within misfortune, good fortune hides."

I threw the book in my cart and moved along.

Reading the Tao Te Ching gave me new thoughts to ponder as I walked. "The source is good and you are born from the source, therefore you are good."

I liked that. I could handle feeling that I was good.

"Water stays low and soft and always beats out what is hard." I reminded myself of this often: stay soft, stay low. Reading the Tao helped open me up to the lessons of nature, and I searched for my own while on my walks.

A magnificent thing about Connecticut that I did not remember ever seeing as a child in Pennsylvania was the sunflowers. I'm not talking about just any kind of sunflowers. I am talking about ten-foot-tall sunflowers with faces the size of dinner plates and big, bright yellow petals the size of corncobs. I was fascinated by these sunflowers and would drive past peoples' homes just to see them and show the kids. And then it dawned on me to grow them myself. So for $1.99, I purchased a package of Mammoth Organic sunflower seeds and sprinkled them beneath the earth right across the driveway from Martha. The rain and sun did their thing, and before we knew it, we had gigantic sunflowers over ten feet tall in our garden. I loved watching the bumblebees fly from flower to flower, and loved that Martha got to watch them all day long. How was it possible that I could plant a few little seeds and now this?

But it kept getting better. It may have been something I should have learned in sixth-grade science class if I had been paying attention, but soon I noticed the heads of the sunflowers moving. In the morning they would be facing one direction, and in the afternoon they would be facing another.

"It's called heliotropism, Mom. It's when the head of the flower moves from east to west, tracking the sun," Jack said in response to my amazement.

"Well, I don't know that fancy name, but I must say I'm quite impressed with this process," I replied.

I was very impressed with this process; how amazing that a flower could move so much in one day. After my walks, I would sit with Martha and watch them, trying to catch them in motion. I never did, but I did think about what was going on. The sun was so warm and comforting, no wonder the flowers wanted to follow him. I thought about people who were like the sun, the ones who never complained and always had smiles on their faces, and I thought about how other people loved to be with them and follow them.

I did not want to win the "I have the most problems" contest; I did not want anyone's sorrow for the losses anymore. I wanted people to feel warm and comforted with me. So I started making a conscious effort to not talk about my problems, to be happy with people even when I did not want to be. My friend Caroline would tell me that when she left a room, she wanted people to feel like they were dancing, and if she could not bring that energy out with her, she stayed home. I liked this idea and I spoke to the kids about it.

"If you walk outside and the sun is shining to your right and there is a big rain cloud to your left, which direction are you going to walk?"

They all said in unison, "Toward the rain cloud."

CHAPTER 11

Time to Ponder

That autumn in Connecticut taught me the beauty of being calm. I loved to watch how each tree took on its own color and created magnificence with its sister trees; the trees never competed with one another, just complemented each other. I loved how willingly nature let her young fly south for warmth, trusting they would return come spring. And I loved how her rain fell so much softer in autumn. Her moods swing, but her thunderstorms pass and her tears of rain rarely cause destruction. I would walk and then lie with Martha formulating the thoughts that flooded my mind on the trail.

As autumn left us and winter set in with more fury, Mother Nature taught me one of her greatest lessons one morning after a storm. It was a crazy night. The wind and rain were blowing so hard, the house shook. Surprisingly, none of the kids were woken up by the ruckus. Come morning, I could see that all the beautiful, colorful leaves outside my bedroom window had been ripped from the trees the night before. The sky was gray, and the beauty of fall now belonged to yesterday.

I remained in bed thinking about how I welcomed the storm, as it mirrored my heart. My eyes still stung from all the tears they had cried the night before after a dream lifted my veil. I opened them halfway as I fought the urge to sink deeper into the safety of my bed. I lay for a while and thought about how many times I had heard people say, "Life is not always what we planned it to be." I wondered, is it ever what we planned it to be?

Eventually, I got up and I went outside to get the mail. To my amazement, the trees appeared more beautiful than ever. Half of their branches were bare and many of their beautiful leaves lay at their roots. However, the rain had soaked their branches and saturated their trunks to turn them a deep, dark brown, and the contrast against the remaining foliage in reds, oranges, and yellows painted a dramatic vision. And there, Mother Nature left me to ponder: like everyone else in the world, I had endured many storms; was it possible I too could come out more beautiful?

🌱 🌱 🌱

THE YOGA STUDIO was above a pizza parlor. I had no idea on that winter morning that there were different types of yoga, each with its own style and philosophy. I took the space in the back corner of the room, as far away from everyone else as possible. The class, taught by the studio owner, Julie, began with a reflection on letting go. She shared a personal experience she'd had with her mother and father when deciding to become a yoga teacher. I liked this. Then we were asked to chant three *om*s. This freaked me out a little bit. Then we sang a mantra in Sanskrit, "the invocation." Instead of closing my eyes fully, I squinted so I could watch the intensity on the faces of the yogis around me. When class began, I found it harder to keep up than I would ever have believed possible. I had heard yoga was more challenging than it looked, and now I believed it. I also had trouble following all the different poses. Julie was very kind and patient, instructing me quietly when everyone else was holding the proper shape.

At the end of class, we *om*-ed one more time and then bowed to our teacher as she bowed to us. "*Namaste*. The light in me honors the light in you," she said. I loved watching Julie after she bowed *namaste* to the class. She kept her head down while the rest of us sat waiting. I could feel her praying. I wanted to climb into her thoughts for those short moments and experience such devoted faith.

That night, I sat with Billy and Jack eating the pizza I'd brought home while describing the class. "It was really crazy, everyone going, "*Om, om, ommmm!*"

"You shouldn't go if you are going to make fun of them. *Om* is a sacred word for many people," Jack said, always politically correct.

"I am not making fun of them, Jack," I clarified. "I'm just saying it freaked me out a little."

"Are you going back?" Billy asked.

"Oh, definitely. I loved it. Especially the crazy stuff."

🌱 🌱 🌱

EVEN IF I COULD ACCEPT that I could change my life by changing my thoughts, I also accepted that my perception was influenced by circumstances. My perception was much more positive when the sky was blue and the sun was shining. Since the cold kept me from walking, when the kids were at school, I kept returning back to my corner of the yoga studio above the pizza parlor.

I kept to myself and observed. Julie knew all of her students well and what they needed to do in their practice. Many times she told me to stop pushing myself so hard. She would see the frustration on my face as I fell out of a balancing pose again and again, or my disappointment when I couldn't do a new pose introduced to me.

"Forget about everything else and just be present on your mat," she would say. "Empty your mind. If you feel yourself wandering, come back to the room and to your practice."

This was impossible for me to do. When I tried quieting my mind, ideas just flew to my brain. As she was asking me to empty my mind, I was doing some of my best thinking. I noticed that some of the students would keep paper and a pen next to their mats to take notes on the instruction. I began to bring paper and a pen also, but I took notes on the mysteries of life and the path to peace.

"Come to the front of your mats. We are going to work on a balancing pose called Tree Pose," Julie said one day as we finished working through some standing poses.

Tree Pose? That sounds right up my alley, I thought, and moved to the end of my mat with enthusiasm.

Julie instructed us to stand still, letting the heaviness of our bodies sink into our mats. Then, shifting our weight to the left, we were to lift our right foot and place it on the inside of our left leg. It was okay to use our hands to assist us as long as we avoided placing our foot on our knee. I loved the idea of this pose.

I quickly lifted my right leg, and with the help of my hands I placed my foot high above my knee and quickly fell forward. *Okay, well that was a surprise*, I thought, and again, I attempted the pose and again fell immediately out of it. I had been a gymnast in my youth, so a lot of yoga poses, like handstands and backbends, came easily to me. Although I was never good on the balance beam, I was surprised and frustrated that I could not balance on one leg for more than two seconds. I looked around the room and saw that most of the other students were happily perched on one leg; some even had their arms extended above their head.

Julie seemed to sense my frustration and gave some pointers without speaking directly to me. "Find a spot on the floor in front of you and stay focused on it. Stay centered; relax your mind."

"A focused, centered, and relaxed mind—if I had all of that, I wouldn't need yoga," I mumbled as I tried and failed again.

Julie moved the class on to the next sequence of poses. I was not ready to move forward. This Tree Pose was so far the most challenging pose I had run up against in class, and I wanted to "win" it.

When I pulled up in the driveway, I almost felt frustrated by Martha's standing there, so tall and confident, on one leg. I got out of the car and looked at her, amazed by how tall she stood in the sky, reaching for the heavens with a trunk no wider than a car tire.

"Martha, what the fuck?"

I knew I could google how she did it and learn all about her root system, but I liked to sense Martha, feel Martha. There's little room for science when you are talking to a tree.

🌳 🌳 🌳

"Martha, I had the best sex last night.

"Oh, please! I know what you are thinking: 'Why do you have to talk about sex so much? Obviously you don't have it enough if you have to talk about it so much, blah, blah, blah.'

"Well, Rich may agree, but how do you even reproduce? Drop a cone somewhere and a boy tree saps on it?"

As we got older, I had to spare some of my girlfriends who were good at visualization and stop talking about sex with them so much. Picturing Rich and myself in bed was painful even for me. We certainly were no Brad and Angelina. But I didn't care about that anymore. Long gone were the days when a ripped stomach and big arm muscles were what I found attractive. Now sexy to me was a man who got his tired ass out of bed every morning to work for me and my kids. Sexy was trust and devotion. Sexy was someone who always made me feel wanted regardless of my inability to do a Kegel. Of course, a ripped stomach and big arm muscles would be a nice addition to the rest, but certainly were not needed.

It takes a lot to keep a marriage together, and I accept that luck is a big part of it. However, for us, my honesty about men's and women's sexual needs helps the most. At my age, nature couldn't care less if I had sex again. I have served my purpose to procreate, and now she is fine with me tending the garden. However, even with my bodily urges subsiding, I still enjoy sex like I enjoy going to a good movie or a good yoga class.

I have learned that as our estrogen decreases, estrogen in men increases, as if it were transferred in some weird way by us leaving tampons in the bathroom trash over the years. This estrogen increase in men is not necessarily equivalent to a decrease in testosterone; it just makes them more emotional about the sex they are having. What happened to the days when a man would take it when and where he got it? Nowadays, if a woman tries to rush it or sit out the orgasm, feelings of rejection set in like they do in a thirteen-year-old girl who doesn't get invited to a sleepover. Men want it meaningful; they need to feel wanted and desired.

I understand sex is how men feel close; it is how they unwind, detox, and it is how they feel alive and young. But they are also capable of having sex no matter how tired they are; there is little worry about the teenager down the hall who may come looking for a parent's signature. It does not matter if they just watched a documentary on the polar bears being endangered or if their friend just got in a fight with his sister. Having sex may be the one thing men are capable of doing while being 100 percent present in the moment.

My divorced friends yell at me when I talk like this, as if I should be forever grateful for my husband's desire for me every minute. But here's my honesty; here is me not pretending that I'm tired. I can't watch a movie about a man in an iron lung having sex and then jump in bed and not think of him. I can't shut out the rap music playing down the hall, knowing I could not afford the therapy my child would need if he or she heard the bedpost banging against the wall. I can't always be in the moment, participating as if I were meeting my lover in a stairwell for hot, passionate sex. On a school night, I can't find the time or attention it takes to devour sex like a four-course meal. I just can't. I can, however, serve up a slice of pizza most nights of the week.

I was finally able to reach Rich with this language. "If you want a four-course meal, then you are going to have to wait until Saturday night, when I'm rested and relaxed. If you are okay with a slice of pizza, I can serve that up many ways. In fact, I love serving pizza. It is easy and takes little energy from me physically and emotionally. I can have food delivered, warm up the leftovers in the refrigerator, or cook the frozen food in the freezer. But I'm talking cheese pizza, no fancy crap on it, not even sausage or pepperoni; just dough, sauce, and cheese! Just be grateful that you get as much pizza as you do."

With this understanding, everyone's needs are met and there are no resentments. Sex keeps a marriage healthy and happy, so I take it for the team and serve pizza a lot.

Yes, long gone are the days when I would try to compensate for my lack of cooking in the bedroom. Nowadays it's pizza, pizza, pizza. The other day I was thinking about what I would call my vagina if I were to give her a name, and the first name that came to me was Marge. Marge—not Lola or Sadie, Destiny or Giselle, but Marge. That's usually not a good sign to want to call your vagina Marge, but it was becoming true for me that sex as I got older just did not work as well as it had when I was younger. I always watched those commercials about women complaining sex hurt as they were heading toward menopause thinking, *Liars—you just don't feel like banging your husband anymore.*

I used to try much harder. I once read a book about a monastic nun in the fourteenth century who requested she be buried in the undergarments she died in. However, an outbreak of the plague at the time of her death forced the convent to undress her, only to find a serpent tattooed down the center of her body. I thought that was fabulous. So for Rich's birthday, I had a henna tattoo of a snake painted down the front of me. The tail started around my nipple and the head lead to my—one time only—perfectly waxed genitalia. It was a delightful gift, but it kept me on top for the next two weeks, which does nothing for me. When I'm on top, I catch myself counting or thinking about something like why the neighbor's tulips bloom so much earlier in the season than mine.

Yes, those were the days that regardless of my grief or how many babies were sleeping in the house, Mother Nature gave me enough energy and desire to keep it fun and exciting.

"I can hear you under your breath, Martha, 'There she goes about sex again.' I may admit I don't have it as much as I may think, but I definitely have it more than Rich thinks. I'm not stupid. I know the rules. When I hear women talking about not having sex often, I want to scream, 'News alert, men fuck.' I was thinking of starting a T-shirt line that stated it. I tell young wives this too. I try not to on business trips, but sometimes it slips out if we are drinking wine. 'Feed them at home, so they don't want to eat at the neighbor's.' Of course, there will be those who are well fed at home and still eat at the neighbor's, but that is a different topic. Another thing I tell young wives is sometimes it's good to hit it up before you go out on a Saturday night to take the pressure off the night. This is especially true at hotels.

"Don't tell Rich I'm telling you any of this, Martha, because he will get all offended, but I swear men think it is in the hotel contract that sex is guaranteed nightly. As if it's unheard of to pay for a hotel and not have sex every night."

I took a moment to reflect.

"Martha, admit it. You think I'm funny."

🌳 🌳 🌳

ONE STUNNING MORNING, the birds were chirping outside my window and the breeze that passed through the room was brilliant. Three tall trees sat directly outside my bedroom window. During the winter they were bare and I could see all the way down the road, but now they were filled out and shaded my room. I had been watching them closely every day for the past two weeks. I had a front-row seat to magic. Stark and brittle all winter, they had gotten a little softer each day, and then one dawn I woke to a hint of life, tiny green buds. I had watched them grow just a little bit bigger every day until they blossomed right in front of my eyes into beautiful white trees. They stayed white for less than three weeks, but for those three weeks they were masterpieces, fantastical extensions to my bedroom.

Bobby had soccer on this morning, so I made my way to the bathroom as he came running in. I was listing all the things he might need. "Do you have your cleats? And make sure you grab a water bottle."

"Mommy, Martha is getting married!"

"What do you mean?"

"Wait 'till you see her. She changed to get married!"

I walked out the front door to get a better look at Martha. Bobby ran by my side, happy to show me.

"See, I told you!"

He was right, I had missed it the spring before, but she did look like she was getting married, with little white flowers scattered throughout her skirt. She was beautiful; she was happy.

"Martha, what a beautiful bride you make.

"You know, Rich and I were engaged within a year and married within the next, with a baby on the way six weeks later. And then married again in front of forty wheelchairs at my grandmother's nursing home. I had promised her if she were alive when I got married, she would be there. She was not healthy enough to travel, so we bought the wedding to her. That day's entertainment was bingo in room B or the wedding in the cafeteria.

"All we knew then was good and easy. Our bodies were healthy and full of energy, our careers were moving forward, and there were no mortgages or bills stressing us out. We had made a commitment to spend the rest of our lives together based on a year's worth of sex and partying and fun. The greatest stress we shared was deciding where to go for dinner. Okay, well I did buy two baby ducklings and let them live in our bathroom and run around the bedroom. It took a bit for Rich to adjust to that, but eventually they got big enough for me to put in the pond nearby.

"Martha, you know how important I think sex is to a marriage, but something hit me the other night. Rich and I were at a restaurant in town, and there were a handful of other couples there. When Rich went to the bathroom, I looked around and tried to assess the group. I may have been wrong, but I could tell the ones who were on a date, a first date, and then those who were married with children. The body language, the amount of speaking they did with one another, etc., made it obvious. But you know who seemed the happiest?

"Not the single waitress. Actually it was the older couple in the corner. They must have been in their mid-seventies and, I bet, married a long time, because they kind of looked like one another. People do that, they start to look like their dogs and their mates after a while. At their age, I assumed they were over trying to change one another or wondering if there was a better life out there to be lived. They had simply accepted one another, and their love was calm. They were peaceful and loving with one another, just beautiful.

"Acceptance—it's a beautiful thing and it creates beautiful things. It's not about settling, that's not it at all. It is about allowing one another to not be perfect, and being grateful. But marriage is hard. How many of us are really equipped to handle the stresses that come with marriage and children, all the realities of life with deaths and career problems?"

I sat quietly another minute and then smiled at Martha.

"Perhaps you are right; they met on Match.com for the Golden Years, and it was their first date. Yeah, maybe."

Rich and I had our struggles like everyone else, especially early on in Connecticut, but for the most part were pretty happy together. But a happy marriage takes time, effort, and wisdom. For instance, I have learned that it is much better to wait until after sex to tell Rich about Olivia getting a third kitten or Billy kicking a ball through the window, than it is to tell him when he walks in the house after a long day of work.

"Martha, Rich is a wonderful man but he makes a lot of loud noises, which can start a lot of fights. Recently, we were at a movie theater that served food. Rich was working on a Caesar salad, and I swore he was trying to compete for the gold medal in lettuce crunching, but I held my tongue, because once we stayed mad at each other for two days after a lettuce-crunching-at-the-movies episode. It was an intense movie, super intense, and the bad guy was just about to hurt a little girl while the good guy was just about to save her. The whole theater was on pins and needles; you could hear a pin drop, until Rich crunched right in my ear. I cursed at him, which is listed in the not-to-do section in the manual of keeping a marriage happy, but you know I can let my anxiety get the best of me at times."

Yes, so much to work out to keep a marriage healthy. Years ago I demanded that Rich email me his list of requests, thinking that this was a good "keep the marriage happy" strategy. I felt like every time I saw him, the conversation was about what was done or needed to be done. It made me feel like his personal assistant and maid, so emailing me his thoughts was a great solution. And it did work well, until he figured out I forwarded the long list to my friend Mary Jane, who got a good laugh out of it.

Rich is very list-oriented. I'm not. The longest lists come on the nights when he is flying. In the past, a flight across America forced him to stop and unwind and offered me a little freedom. Now with the damn internet, it gives him time to go over all the emails I never responded to. Then he sends questions like, What do you want to do with our future, where do you want to live, how much money should we put away for travel, how often will we visit kids and grandchildren? and so on. I do not know what I'm making for dinner tonight, so emails like this challenge me and usually make their way to Mary Jane before being answered.

🌱 🌱 🌱

I HAD A BEAUTIFUL OLD wooden box where I stored newspaper articles, letters I wrote, and mail I received following the accident. I had opened the box once before, but I was too emotional to really connect with all of its contents. I felt so much stronger now, so decided it was time to revisit those memories.

I had some time while the kids played outdoors, so I went up the stairs to my room. I walked into my closet and reached back behind the shelves that held my sweaters and pulled the chest out. I carried it back into my room. I sat down on the floor and lifted the lid, realizing the contents inside had not been disturbed in ten years.

At first sight, all I saw were scores of sympathy cards, cards with beautiful pictures of nature, religious cards, and cards with inspirational reflections. I began reading one after another: "Words cannot express our sorrow." "We are so sorry about your loss." "Please know you and your family are in our thoughts."

Some of the cards were from people I barely knew; some were from friends I had always known. My friends' relatives sent cards also, and this meant so much to me, because they were unexpected. I regretted all the cards I had thought to send and never had.

The hardest cards to read were those from my closest friends, because I knew they felt my pain. They not only loved me, but they loved my parents as well. Mary Jane wrote, "This is the hardest card for me to send—maybe that is why it has taken me so long. There are no words to express how deeply sorry I am. If I could take away your pain for only a minute, I would. But I know the only thing I can do is be here to listen whenever you need me. Love, Mary Jane."

When I found the card that my friend Janie had stuck in my hands the morning of the service, I was moved beyond words. She had grown up in a family with five children. She never knew her father, who had died young from heart problems. Her mother was at work a great deal of the time trying to support her growing children. I had no idea to what extent my parents had touched Janie's life. I knew they meant a lot to her, but not until I reread her letter did I realize that she loved them so much. She described being heartbroken because she could never let them know how much they touched her life, the simple things like being greeted by my father's warm welcome and my mother's soft touches. She wrote, "Tricia, I never once heard your parents yell at you or say one negative thing to you."

The next letter I read was from a friend I had gone to high school with. He was a very good friend, and when my parents died, he disappeared on me. A month later, he called to tell me he just didn't know what to say. My response was, "Well, this was about me, not you." I was upset, very upset, and I never forgot that he was not there for me when I needed him most. I felt ashamed of myself as I reread his words. I realized he was there for me; it just took him a little time to find his courage. He wrote:

Dear Trish,

My lack of correspondence is inexcusable. I admit my wrong-doing right off the bat, because it bothers me immensely. The event that changed everyone's life is hard to deal with because it happened to a very special, caring and most important, giving person. Trish, I know how much your parents meant to you, especially your mother. I remember you were always talking to her on the phone and just speaking about her in general. I know there was a special bond you guys had, and I will always remember it fondly. Two attributes that you possess are strength and resilience. You've always landed on your feet. Your parents probably handed down this positive characteristic of yours to you. Trish, please know I think about you often.

Love, Peter

What a lovely letter, and I had remembered only the negative. Oh, how the human mind likes to swing to the negative! What a great injustice to my good friend for me to have harbored resent-ment all these years when he had beautifully rectified the situation.

Next, I pulled out a two-page typed letter that I wrote to be read in court during sentencing for the man who killed my parents:

It is hard for me to know where to begin. It is as if I have lived two lives; one started six months ago. Starting with September 16th, I thought life couldn't get worse. Yet to our surprise, life has gotten worse and daily living is sometimes too painful to allow.

The obvious, like Christmas and birthdays, are bad enough. However, it is the times when you go to their house and search for clothes they have worn to smell their scent, or you call their answering machine again and again to hear their voices to have proof of their once existence. These are the times that life is almost unbearable.

I am so different now. A part of my soul has died and is gone forever. I am not the same wife or mother to my family as I once was, and my zest for life has disappeared. My parents were such great parents and great role models. Their abilities to love us unconditionally and teach us good values and morals are what will bring us through this tragedy.

My father was a major in the National Guard and my mother taught special-ed children for twenty years. They were good citizens, who respected their neighbors and did right in their community.

You can ask yourself "What if" a million times when something like this happens but the only "What if" that could have saved my parents lives is "What if" he, Mr. P., shared these same values.

My father was only 54 years old. He was in better health than the average twenty-five-year-old and if his life wasn't cut short, he would have seen me to my 54th birthday. When they died, we not only lost our parents, but our mentors and best friends.

I come here today with my sisters to ask the court to give us justice. Help us move on and begin to heal our lives. We must continue to be good parents to our own children, and teach them good values to live by. We are very confused now, and it is hard to trust in a world where one man's gross negligence can destroy your family. However, in honor of our parents, we will over time stand strong and try our best to be better human beings.

Thank you for your time.

Patricia LaVoice

I can remember clearly now, standing tall in front of the judge just ten weeks pregnant with Billy as I read that letter. My husband, sisters, relatives, and friends all sat in support behind me. What about the man who stood alone in court that day, the man who single-handedly changed so many people's lives with his reckless driving? Was there a chance I had forgotten any attempt he may have made to apologize?

I wrote this letter just six months after their death. Many of my feelings were still the same. The letter showed how much I had healed, but also how little I had healed. I let the accident become me instead of being something that had happened to me. I thought about what I said in court, that in my parents' honor we would try to be better human beings, and I was pleased.

I continued searching through the box and came across a clear plastic bag. As I lifted it, I could see a small brown hairbrush. My stomach sank and tears immediately flowed. Here in my hand, I held physical proof of my mother's existence. Her soft brown hair that I had run my fingers through so many times covered the brush. I loved her hair—its touch, its smell, its look. She always had it fixed with a little bit of a soft curl to it. It reached just below her shoulders, perfectly framing her beautiful face.

I cried hard as I held the bag close to my chest. How remarkable and startling that my mother had died over a decade ago, but I had her hair in my hands. I thought about removing the hair from the bag and holding it, smelling it, feeling it. I left it as it was.

As I placed the plastic bag back into the corner of my box, I saw a note. I unfolded the pages and began to read the rawest words I have ever written in my life. I had put them to paper for my parents' memorial forty-eight hours after their death. I was not physically or mentally strong enough to read it, so after his father sang the *Ave Maria*, Rich stood in front of the packed church and did it for me. He stood at the podium crying as he read:

> *Our hearts have been broken and life has shown us how fragile it can be. I wanted to talk a little about my parents so you can all take a part of them home with you today. I fear the future and the pain it will bring, and I search desperately to understand why this has happened. I want to go on living as my parents would want, and I ask them for the strength to help me be more loving and giving than ever before. My parents, as you all know, were truly great people. They were friends to us kids, and they*

became close to our friends in turn. They respected the lives of everyone around them. My father taught us girls many things about life. He taught us how to appreciate the beauty of nature, like how the trees would cast a beautiful shadow in the autumn light. He taught us to be respectful of all living things. He taught us not to kill an insect, for all living things deserve respect. My dad was always making sure we felt good about ourselves and told all of us girls repeatedly how proud of us he was. He never held back his words of love and taught us how important it is to let those around you know how much you care. He loved my mother so much and made her feel special every day. My dad was a wonderful husband and father. As for my mother, well I don't think my heart will allow me at this time to look too deeply. Everyone who knew her, knew she was special. She was a symbol of maternal love. She was the best mother in the world. She was my best friend and I will give back to her by trying to be as good a mother as I can be. Bill and Pat Lanahan, what wonderful souls. I see them now holding hands roaming through heaven.

They are together and at peace and I am happy for that. My heart hurts most for my daughter and nieces and nephews. My parents lived every day to make life as beautiful as possible for their grandchildren. I am glad they touched the children's lives

~~as they did, but it was unfairly cut too short. I have learned so~~

much from their unconditional love, as I hope all of you have. I will miss their sense and their laughter. We will all miss them beyond words and love them so deeply.

Love, Tricia

I reached down into the box again and came up with two samples of my parents' handwriting I had saved. I vaguely remembered taking them off their kitchen table when I went back to their house to pack up their things. My father's writing was a neat box print, and his words spoke of work-related plans for the upcoming months. My mother's writing was a beautiful flowing cursive that graced the page of notes from what I thought was an English class she had been taking at the local community college. The paper was small, the size of a notepad one would keep next to the phone. As I read her words, it became clear that she had actually been studying ancient Greek history. I loved this, because Olivia was studying Greek history in school and was very passionate about the subject. I flipped the page over and read my mother's words on the back: "There is not, and never will be, an explanation of human suffering that man's intelligence can comprehend."

I do not know who she was quoting, but how amazing! I had so few of my mother's written words, and these were among them.

And there in the box was the newspaper article that I would not look at in the days following the accident. Trying to avoid the picture of their car crushed like a beer can, I skimmed the article. My head spun reading that my parents had been turning at the light when he smashed into them. So many years fearing red lights, and this was not even how it had happened.

I had emptied my box with the exception of one small card with a picture of the Madonna on its cover. It was, by far, the most gorgeous portrayal I had ever seen of her.

Her delicate fingers rested on her chest, where they were met with the glow of her heart. Her mesmerizing eyes appeared soft and gentle, yet pierced straight into mine. I felt comforted by it until I turned it over.

"Oh, fuck," I said out loud. This was not a letter of condolence. It was my parents' Mass card, one of the many the church had handed out to guests as they entered the church for my parents' memorial service. How had it made its way into my box? I had never seen it before. I was sure of it. The heading read: "In loving memory of Patricia A. Lanahan and William V. Lanahan." Under that it read, "Died September 17th, 1993." It sickened me to read their names, and that feeling quickly turned to disbelief and near anger as I read the poem that followed:

There's a Reason *(Romans 8:26)*
For every pain that we must bear,
For every burden, every care,
There's a reason.
For every grief that bows the head,
For every teardrop that is shed,
There's a reason.
For every hurt, for every plight
For every lonely, pain racked night,
There's a reason.
But if we trust God as we should
It all will work out for our good.
He knows the Reason.

I was speechless, confused, and angry. I closed the box and went outside to sit with Martha.

"Martha, when you lose someone you love, time is meaningless—four minutes, four days, four years. Immediately after the accident, it was suggested that I take some antianxiety drugs to take the edge off my pain. I understood it worked for some people, and I respected their choice, but I was okay with being in pain. I was supposed to be in pain. Everyone would try hard to talk to me about everything but the accident, and that was all I wanted to talk about. It occupied every corner of my mind. They were the ones who were uncomfortable talking about it. When I spoke of my parents and started to cry, I always said, 'Please be okay with my tears.'"

I felt a wish forming within me:

I remember a time when pain meant scraping your knee against the pavement, problems were solved in math class, and loss existed only on fliers posted on telephone poles for a missing pet. Our greatest worry was catching the ice cream truck. Our greatest conflicts were over the rules in a game of hide-and-seek. Life was magical and full of wonder. We could have no more conceived of the challenges we would face in the years to come than we could of how the sandman got into our house every night. Pain, worry, conflict sneak up on us in adult sizes not concerned about rules, fair or unfair. We learn that pain is as much a part of adulthood as play is of childhood. That problems cannot be solved if they are not faced, and the first thing we lose trying to hide from the pain is ourselves. To seek happiness is not enough; we must have courage and strength to address our problems, face our pain, even when it feels like an unfair game. Then we can see clearly that much of life still remains magical and wondrous. I wish for you courage and strength.

"I have never believed that there is a bright side to everything, Martha. Some things just suck. But I do believe we can learn something from every experience. We have the power to make good out of what we have learned. They say, 'What does not kill you will make you stronger.' My friend, Caroline from Los Angeles would say, 'What does not kill you almost kills you.' It takes a lot of strength and courage to walk through pain, and it is easier to stay a victim rather than fight to be a survivor. I do not think we always realize there is a difference between the two—and you can say this about all hardships of life. We all have them; mine was just easier for the world to see."

ˏ   After my parents were killed, I had to work very hard to get myself to a place where I did not expect tragedy every time the phone rang. I had lost my false sense of security—the idea that bad things couldn't happen to me. It became essential for me to be prepared for the next catastrophe, to know I could survive it. I still have a perfect plan if I lose Rich on the way home from work. I know whom I will call, what I will tell the children, and what I will need to sell. I had thought and thought about how I would handle the next possible death in my life, and then the phone rang, this time about Aaron. So all my neuroses were properly fueled; any trust I had gained was lost. I know this is unhealthy, but I am working on it. Healing takes time. I allow myself some neuroses. I expect neuroses. I think the most valuable thing I have gained by tragedy is the understanding that at any time you can lose those you love. It is no longer something that happens to other people on the news.

Time helps you accept death, but to think you get over it is as silly as thinking you will get over someone's cutting your arm off. Sure, you will adapt—but you will never wake up one morning and say, "I didn't need that arm anyway."

And no matter how much time passes, there will be days your missing limb will ache.

It takes the mind a great deal of time to adjust to death. In the beginning of your adjustment to your new reality, your day-to-day life mirrors the experience of a child who has been injured and is holding her breath. She is impossible to console, so you just wait for the scream. Once the scream has found its way out, you must give it its time. There is so little comforting that you can do at this juncture. So you wait for the whimpering and then hopefully she will let you look at her wound. She will pull back and tell you not to touch, she will fight your love and your desire to heal her, but you must persevere.

❦ ❦ ❦

YOGA CLASS BEGAN and Julie reminded us that this was our practice; it was not a competition and we should not worry about what our neighbor was doing on the mat next to us.

"If you need to rest, take Child's Pose," she said, looking directly at me.

Julie sat quietly before beginning her talk. I was anxious to hear what she would say this morning. She seemed to be on a roll. The week prior, she had offered the best explanation for loneliness that I had ever heard. She said the purpose of loneliness was to return us to our source—that only going inward will release us from the pain. The more I studied nature, the more I felt that anything universal had to serve a purpose; something as powerful and vile as loneliness certainly had to serve a purpose. I stored her explanation in my mind's Loneliness file, along with my thought that it forced us back to the pack to stay safe from predators.

Julie took a deep breath and began.

"This morning I would like us to focus on negative self-talk and the negative voices in our own head. The voices that make us doubt ourselves or even loathe ourselves. When you fall out of a pose, watch your thoughts. If you can't hit a pose, what are you thinking about yourself?"

She spoke as if everyone in the room had negative voices in their head. Like it was normal. I knew I had them—but not until that moment did I feel separated from them and able to exert control over them. They were like a bad habit, like picking at a cut. You did it so often, you forgot you were doing it at all, until someone told you to stop.

A wonderful and powerful statement I recently read by Anaïs Nin moved me greatly. She wrote, "And the day came when the risk to remain tight in a bud was more painful than the risk it took to blossom."

The use of the word "risk" was where this quote hit me. She did not write just "to blossom"; she wrote "the risk it took to blossom"— an amazing insight that this author verbalized so many years ago. I got it. I knew I was a bud. I have always been a safe, tight bud. My parents took care of me, Rich took care of me, and then Terese and Barbara took care of me. And I was always one to put my friends on a pedestal. I grew up idolizing my sister Liz so badly, my seventh-grade friends threatened to dump me if I did not stop talking about her and her friends. I carried on this way in life, always finding mentors that could do no wrong. I idolized Terese, and I put Barbara up so high, I don't know how she managed to breathe the thin air.

Just days after my parents' death, I promised myself that I would be better for having lost them, and love more. I did feel more loving towards others, but what about towards myself? I wanted to be free—free of fear, of anxiety, and mostly of the thoughts that were holding me back. But it was time I had the courage to face myself and love myself. I knew I was not on this journey alone—obviously not, or yoga classes across the world would not be filled and Anaïs Nin's sentiment would not be famous. We all have fears and suffering and painful memories; mine were just easier to see in their black-and-white form called death. But that made me no different than the woman who quietly held shame from an abuse, or the man who felt like a failure for never having lived up to his father's standards. As my father taught me as a little girl, we are all much more alike than we let on. Some hold their pain in and suffer alone for a lifetime, some self-medicate and never recognize it, and some will look at it and try their best to release it.

As I practiced that morning, I was very conscious to stay kind and forgiving with myself. When I left the studio I noticed that the whole class looked lighter, happier. Where negative self-talk comes from or why we do it remained a mystery to me. I could not have been raised with more positive reinforcement from my parents. But I was aware of it now; it was another of life's universal ills. Maybe it was the meaning of life, what makes life a journey, the road to forgiving and loving oneself.

When I got home, I asked Martha why people engage in negative self-talk. And within me arose a wish, almost in response:

It patiently awaits you like spring yearning to be birthed
through a winter's frost. It has always been there and always
will be. The fortunate will discover it quickly but others may
resist it, feeling undeserving and go a lifetime in the absence of its
glory. Nevertheless, it is there within all of us. A time, a moment,
when we simply let go and love ourselves. We forgive our faults,
accept our limitations, and stop looking for inadequacy within.
A realization that makes self-doubt appear uninteresting,
almost indulgent as we recognize we, ourselves, are worthy of
the same respect we give others. This moment may come to you
in beauty like a bird waking the forest with song. Yet, it may
come in thunder when you desperately need love and the only

one capable of delivering it is you. Allow the moment; know it is waiting. No matter how long or harsh the winter blows, spring always appears. Believe that within you, no matter how harsh your self-doubt, lies a spring of self-love yearning to be birthed.

For you, I wish self-love.

🌱 🌱 🌱

"Martha, when Olivia gets her period, I'm flying her to California and we are going to have a big Red Tent party with all my friends. I'm going to rent Moroccan tents and have everyone dress up as if in biblical times and we are going to celebrate her power to now procreate. Oh please, Martha, don't you get on the "poor Rich" train too. He should have known things would be different with me. When we were dating, I used to turn around and talk to our imaginary children in the back seat. If he married a woman who did that, then I do not feel sorry for him."

🌱 🌱 🌱

In the winter months, I struggled with my perception. The sky darkened before I had finished carpooling in the afternoon, and everyone was just tired and grumpy. Without my walks, my ass grew bigger and my mind smaller. I would talk to Sheila on the phone as she walked along the beach in shorts. I understood that my surroundings influenced my perception, but still it did not matter. When you are in it, you are in it.

One cold Friday night, Rich's friend Steven came over to play chess. The kids were scattered throughout the house unwinding from a week of school. I knew the yoga studio had a guest teacher conducting a weekend seminar, and I decided I would attend the opening Friday-evening class. When I arrived, the students were everywhere. I had never seen the studio so packed. I felt a slight panic when I looked to the back-left corner, my sanctuary, and it was coated in yoga mats. And then I heard a familiar voice.

"Tricia, over here. Join us."

I looked over to see Julie and a few other familiar faces.

"Come, we can make space."

They began moving their mats around, opening up a spot right next to Julie. Everything in my body wanted to turn around and walk out that door. I smiled and squeezed my mat in between their mats, leaving as much room between myself and Julie as possible—which was about three inches.

A thin, cheery man with curly blond hair stood in front of us. He spoke of life from a place where Cheerios and rainbows meet. He introduced his wife and spoke of her as being from a place where goddesses and mothers meet. And then he instructed the class to chant three *om*s, followed by the invocation. I did not want Julie to know I mocked this part of the class, so I hummed on the first *om*, but I could not ignore the beautiful harmony of all the voices coming together. On the second *om*, I gave in and quietly chanted along. I was self-conscious with Julie at my side but quickly realized that she was there as a student and not interested in what was happening on anyone's mat but her own. On the third *om*, I sang from my gut and felt something inside of me open up.

The class began singing the invocation, and the room felt enchanted. I stayed quiet to take it in. Voices harmonized like angels thanking the gods. It was one of the most beautiful sounds I had ever heard. Then we were instructed to open our eyes, and our physical practice began. We were going to start with a breathing exercise. The teacher instructed us all to pair up with someone and sit on the ground back to back. He and his wife demonstrated the drill: while sitting with your backs pressed together, interlocking your elbows with your partner, you were to find a rhythm of simultaneously breathing in and out. When one of you was letting out air, the other person was taking it in and then vice versa. This was way beyond my comfort zone, breaking all my intimacy boundaries, so I got up and quietly went to the bathroom. I planned to stay there long enough for everyone to find a partner, especially Julie, and then rejoin the class when this exercise was over.

I gave it a good couple of minutes, the normal time allocated to pee and wash my hands, and headed back to my mat.

When I returned, the room was filled with laughter and chatter as everyone continued to get in position. I was relieved to see everyone paired up and felt proud of myself for escaping. I returned to my mat and watched until the unthinkable happened: the teacher saw me partnerless and came over to my mat to buddy up with me. We sat back to back, his elbows wrapped through mine, his back pressing against mine. "Okay, when you feel me breathe in, you breathe out. And I will breathe out when you breathe in. Ready?"

Shit.

We began taking turns breathing in and out, feeling one another's spinal cord flattening against our own, becoming one in breath. We did this for about a minute, and then he released his arms and stood up. I joined him standing, and he thanked me with grateful eye contact before returning to his place in front of the class. Surprisingly, no one seemed to notice that I had just had this uncomfortable experience. No one was interested in me. They were all enjoying their own experiences and personal growth. Again, for the second time that night I felt a small shift in my ability to open up.

That night when I lay with the kids rubbing their backs before bed, I told them about my night. Bobby thought it sounded cool and asked if he could take yoga. Jack had little response. Billy had a friend over, so he passed on his backrub. And Olivia knew me well enough to find the whole thing funny.

"Haha! You must have died when you saw him heading over to you! I wish I was there to watch."

I left out the part about feeling an opening up of my heart as I left the studio that night. She would ridicule me, and I was not providing the ammunition.

🌱 🌱 🌱

"MARTHA, NOT TO BE HYPOCRITICAL about God doing things without a reason, but don't you think He put hair on our bodies for a reason and doesn't want us taking it off? I don't have time to keep the hair off my big toes, so I'm hardly worried about keeping the rest of me trim."

Rich knows not to ask me about the grooming stuff; it usually doesn't go too well for him. The other night when I entered the bedroom undressed, he casually asked, looking directly at my crotch, "Do many of your friends shave?" I don't know how many vaginas Rich thinks I see to report back about, but I knew that was not the purpose of his asking. He just wanted to ease into suggesting that I shave, without my biting his head off. I gave the best reply I had: "Not sure, Rich. The only one I know for sure who waxes is your sister." That quieted him up.

Once, he cautiously suggested we shave as foreplay—he would do it for me! Last time I'd checked, hand-eye coordination only declined with age, so letting a man wearing bifocals anywhere near my labia with a razor blade was as likely a scenario for foreplay as bringing home the cute waitress.

"Oh, I know you get sick of hearing about sex, but roll with it or stand still with it, whatever trees do. Girlfriends talk about sex, and you are now my girlfriend. Actually, Martha, you are my best friend now."

Y Y Y

RICH AND STEVE WALKED into the house one day, talking about their plans for the afternoon. It was becoming routine that the kids would head out to their friends' houses or friends would come over on the weekends. Likewise, Steve would come by ours, and he and Rich would fix things. Steve was handy and Rich was not but made a good apprentice. After they hammered this and painted that, there was always a game of tennis followed by some chess. "Tricia, we are going to paint the shed and then remove the vines around Martha," Rich said.

"What are you talking about?" I said, freezing in place.

Steve, unaware of the forbidden territory he was entering, elaborated. "That big pine tree at the end of your driveway? It is covered in vines that will kill—"

"Not a chance you are touching her!" Emotion overcame me so quickly, I surprised myself. I lowered my head to hide my tears.

"Tricia, if you care about Martha, you want to take care of her, right?" Rich asked.

"I want to take care of her, but I don't want to give her a sex change. I don't want Martha to be Marty tomorrow," I hollered, grabbing my yoga mat from the table before turning back to them. "Schedule some other thing to fix. I do not want you messing with Martha. I will call a tree person, an expert, before anyone touches her skirt."

While signing in at the yoga studio, I could not help myself from talking about Martha. I did not hold back my tears either. Everyone was understanding and lovely, and then one woman I did not know asked a very important question.

"Does she flower?"

"Yes, every spring she gets beautiful little white flowers all over her skirt."

"She is fine. Her ivy will not hurt her." She went on to explain the different kinds of ivy and which ones can hurt a tree, but I was too thrilled to comprehend much of what she was saying after I heard, "Her ivy will not hurt her."

Her ivy will not hurt her. No one will hurt her.

🌳 🌳 🌳

MY LAST SEPTEMBER IN LOS ANGELES, I had written simple wishes to give back to Barbara. Now, as I continued to write them, I could feel my writing shaped by the openness of the thoughts that my walks and readings had offered me. As the days went by, the wishes just seemed to flow into my mind and take form as I walked in nature. I often sent them to Barbara and she suggested I print them or at least share them with others.

Leeza was in New York filming a commercial, and she invited me to dinner in Manhattan. On my way into the city, I studied the beauty outside my train window and also all the graffiti and litter. The dichotomy of the world we lived in swirled in my thoughts as another wish took form.

At dinner, Leeza and I discussed the wish, and she asked me to send it to her once I finished writing it. So I sent the wish to Leeza, along with a few others I had already shared with Rich.

I found I could speak to people honestly through the wishes. And the best part of sharing them with Rich was that he could listen to me without feeling a need to fix me. I was lonely, and I had to handle that on my own, and find my own way back to me. Just like a baby bird recently pushed from the nest, confused about why until she realizes she has the power to fly—that's why. I was still flapping my wings, but I was determined to fly on my own. My only other choice was to fall, and I had too wonderful a life not to fly.

Having a focus, something that belonged to me, felt good. I would walk and write a wish for the different people in my life and share them with my family and closest friends.

🌳 🌳 🌳

THERE WERE MANY THINGS I had missed about the East Coast when living on the West one—like a good bagel and a slice of New York pizza. But hands down, what I missed the most was the thunderstorms. The kids had never experienced anything like them, so it was always so thrilling when the lightning and thunder began pounding down. Sometimes the lightning would get so close to the house, I would force the kids into the basement with flashlights, but many times we would sit in the window and watch the sky's magic.

It rained so much harder out East and I loved, loved, loved to walk in the pouring rain. I know this confused some of our neighbors, because on many clear summer evenings, I would walk with an umbrella, because I was deathly afraid of the bats overhead. I tried hard to get out and get my work done in the morning or afternoon, but sometimes I just could not get to it until the evening. So on many dry, warm nights I carried an umbrella, and on the pouring, rainy nights I walked with my face up to the sky.

One night, our neighbor pulled over and insisted I get in his car. I explained I enjoyed the rain, but he lectured me on the dangers of the lightning that I could not see and the thunder I could not hear at the time. I hated it. I felt like such a damsel in distress being rescued by the big strong neighbor, but I did not want to be rude. He seemed to truly care, so I got into his car, soaking the seat.

🌳 🌳 🌳

ONE FRIDAY EVENING in late summer, Olivia was out with friends. We had just begun to allow her to drive with friends and to allow her to drive her friends. She had an eleven o'clock curfew that I was pretty strict about. Of course, being the oldest, Olivia got the toughest parenting; for example, not being allowed to watch PG-13 movies until she was thirteen, while the boys enjoyed much more freedom.

Around ten thirty that evening, it began to rain. I texted Olivia and told her to head home now but to make sure her friend drove very carefully. She texted back that they were just finishing up something to eat and would head home. Around ten fifty it began to pour so hard, it sounded like the roof was going to collapse. Normally, I would love an evening such as this, but I got crazy with worry. Our home was less than a mile from the base of the mountain, which Olivia would be on right about now. I wanted to call her or text her, but I did not want to add any more distraction to the drive. All I could do was pray and pace. It seemed the faster I walked in circles, the harder the rain fell.

Around ten past eleven, when she was still not home, Rich began to question me about where she was and who was driving and so on. His nervous energy just added to my stress, because he never worried. I went into her bedroom and sat in the windowsill, where I could see down the street and look at Martha. I was almost too choked up with anxiety and crazy thoughts to even acknowledge

Martha, but I did. "Oh, Martha, tell God I will do anything. Just bring my baby home safely."

Minutes passed by that felt like hours. Then at approximately 11:18 p.m., I saw headlights coming up the street and pulling into our driveway. I yelled out to Rich, "She's home! She's home!" And then I ran downstairs and out the door to greet her. The rain soaked my clothes almost instantly. "Martha, she's home," I said as I waited beside her for Olivia to get out of the car. Her friend parked, and the two girls went running toward the house.

When we got inside, Olivia was just as freaked out as I was. "It was horrible, the scariest night of my life. We couldn't even see to pull over."

I went to bed that night so emotionally exhausted, and repeatedly thanked God for returning her home safely to me. The storm passed and the sun woke us all with his bright yellow light. I cannot recall how I heard the news, but soon the whole town was in mourning. At approximately 11:10 p.m. the previous night, an accident on the mountain had left two teenaged boys badly injured and a teenaged girl dead. I was overwhelmed with sadness.

Why that child? Had God not heard her mother's plea? Was there any reason or sense? Was I to believe it was just this child's time but not Olivia's? Olivia had crossed that same stretch of road just minutes earlier. Was it purely bad driving conditions and bad luck, or had God played a hand in this? I couldn't imagine a god who could inflict such suffering on his children, and yet, how could life be so fragile that a young, beautiful child could be so easily taken by the slip of a wheel?

I walked outside into the morning sun—clear crystal-blue skies, birds singing, and the voices of neighborhood children faint in the background. The only signs of the storm were some broken branches lying on the fresh green grass, soaking up the sun's love. Yet, just miles away, a family was devastated. But the day in front of me paid no attention to that; it just went along with its business.

So much of the peace I had worked so hard to find was gone. I was mad, mad at God, because there didn't seem to be any reason for this devastation. I looked to Martha, who also seemed to be paying no attention, and spoke. "Martha, what the fuck?"

The next day, I walked a trail by the children's school. It allowed me privacy even though it was not too far off the beaten track. I had grabbed a few of Martha's pine cones and tossed them here and there along my walk. This was the only trail I ventured on that had a finished path for bike riders. In springtime I would be conscious to avoid stepping on all the new life that crawled along the path. Now the only sign of nature's creatures was those dried and flattened to the cement. I pondered all the caterpillars that had crawled across this path and then turned into beautiful butterflies off to Florida or Mexico. But why did these few lie before me, flattened to the pavement? Survival of the fittest? I did not think so; they looked fat and healthy. God's plan? Could God actually decide which caterpillars made it to be butterflies and which got hit by a bicycle? Did God have it in his plan to get Olivia home safely the night before, while the other child lost her life? That was hard for me to accept.

I walked some more, holding the last of Martha's pine cones. I got to the end of my trail and turned around. After walking a few yards, I spotted a place in the forest that appeared magical, darkened by the thicket of bush surrounding it. Moss covered much of it. The birds sang and crickets chirped. It was a perfect place to leave Martha's pine cone. I pulled my arm way back and with all my might I released Martha's pine cone to the warm summer air, watching it fly through the sky before softly landing in a perfect place in the perfect forest.

I walked some more thinking about how much I had grown since all the losses. I wondered who I would have become without them. I thought about all the people who had entered my life and the roles they played. My loss was my greatest teacher. The pain did offer me great clarity. However, I would not accept there was a reason for everything. It was my decision to make the best out of my pain, my decision to try to make their deaths count. And I would not have done anything differently even if I were convinced there was a reason. The benefits from my loss were by choice, my choice. And more important, there were people whose lives held greater suffering than mine. Who was I to think God had a plan for their despair? God showed me a lot through nature, but God never called me up and said, "Hi, Tricia, yeah I do it all for a reason. Go with it."

I felt a deep pain in my heart as I realized that every time I got closer to believing that things happened for a reason, that God had a plan, I saw despair and lost my faith in this notion. I wanted an answer. I wanted to believe there was a reason behind all the suffering in the world. If I believed this, I could get rid of the fear of tragedy's striking again. But the suffering of the world has been just too great for me to think God has a plan. I feared I could never be at peace without an answer. I felt utter hopelessness.

Now I walked alone, letting my mind spin, when an epiphany swept me off my feet. What if I did not need an answer, what if I just let go? I could trust God enough to surrender to what would be, regardless if there was a reason or not. I would stop needing an answer. I would stop becoming frustrated when other people talked about "God's reason" and simply respect that their beliefs were right for them. I wanted to let go.

Suddenly, I felt lifted, aware that even in stillness, time moves and I am a fool to tread in bitterness. I do not hold myself as "enlightened" but as "in search."

> *I breathe deep, then deeper, and then I breathe again. I follow the soft flow of my breath as I inhale and exhale, noticing the steady rhythm that calms me. It is there in this perfect exchange of give and take that life reminds me to give out exactly what I wish to take in. If I proceed with hostility, judgment, and resentment, then it is hostility, judgment, and resentment that will find me. If I proceed with love, trust, and gratitude, then it is love, trust, and gratitude that will find me. Therefore, I write the lyrics to*

*the song I wish to sing. I create the harmony and rhythm in my
life and I proceed, giving out exactly what I seek to take in. Like
the perfect breath that sustains you, I wish for you the song you
wish to sing.*

🌾 🌾 🌾

IN LIFE, I FELT I HAD GIVEN the sun the right amount of attention. I
appreciated a nice sunny day at the beach. I wore sunscreen, and I
put on a sweater when the sun set. In my high school years, I stayed
up a few times to watch the sun rise over the Atlantic, and when I
lived in California, I watched it set on the Pacific.

We miss things more when we do not have them. That's what
it was like for me when I moved to Connecticut. Connecticut is not
known for its lack of sun, but the town we lived in was in a valley,
and we got many cloudy days. I might not have noticed this so much
if I had not just come from Santa Monica, where the sun dances in
the sky 95 percent of the year.

I did not want to mention the lack of sun to anyone, out of fear
this would just add to the list of "Tricia's complaints about Connecticut" that people were sick of hearing. Actually, I was not even sure
if it was all in my mind or not. Maybe I was just finding the negative
anywhere I could to justify my unhappiness. Then one day, Bobby
asked me two very important questions from the back seat of the car.

"Mom, why do we have skin?"

I replied, "It keeps our bodies together and protects us. Just think
if you did not have it, your guts and all would fall out all over the car
seat."

He laughed and continued, "Gross! Why does God not make the
sun shine here?" Yes, there it was! Right out of the mouth of a babe.
I wasn't crazy.

Once I adapted to the overcast days of our town, I came to appreciate a sunny day much more. But beyond that, I knew the sun had a
lot to teach me. Mother Nature was opening my eyes to so much, and

the sun was one of her biggest achievements. I was certain the sun was male, the sky female, and most bodies of water female.

A beautiful thing I noticed about the sun was that he did not exclude or judge anyone. He did not care what color you were, how old you were, what you drove, if you were a kind, honest human being or a criminal. He shone down equally on everyone. I loved his refusal to discriminate, and I loved his thinking that everyone was deserving of warmth. He also did something just as amazing as that. If you closed your eyes and directed your face right at him, no matter where you were standing, in a ghetto or a palace, he made you feel like you were the only one he was shining on. It was beautiful, and I yearned to love this way, to love each person in my life with such focused energy that they felt like they were the only ones I was loving at that moment.

When I tried it, surprisingly, it was not that hard. Everyone feels special and good when shown love. I knew I could not show my love if I were not present, so I tried to focus more on listening and not talking about my life. I just did my best to love everyone as much as I could.

Although a lesson in unconditional love is priceless, personally I needed to learn something more important from the sun. I needed to learn to pray and be thankful on a regular basis. I thought about sunrises and sunsets—the brilliant colors, the magical moments, and the romance they can inspire. I thought a lot about sunsets and sunrises, and I watched them very carefully—of course many more sunsets than sunrises.

One evening while watching the sun settle in the west, I bowed goodnight and wrote a wish to help me fully appreciate and grasp the intensity. I could not believe I had taken the sun's actions for granted every day of my life.

If you are awake, you can see him glowing the moment before he begins his morning rise over the earth's crust. It will take him most of the day to ascend, but it is in those two minutes at sunrise while he hugs the earth that you can feel his devotion the most. Then, after his day's work is complete, he will mesmerize you once more as he slowly descends. However, it is in those final two minutes as he hugs the earth's crust that you can feel his gratitude the most, trusting his return to love again tomorrow. I study him rising and falling, hoping to be awakened in my own life and to love my day through. I study him rising and falling, understanding the significance of starting each day with two minutes of devotion, ending each night with two minutes of gratitude. I study his rise and fall and wish to warn those around me wishing to make my world a brighter place. For you, I wish the sun's love.

I challenged myself to stay in bed every morning and lie still for two minutes, thinking of everything I was grateful for in my life. And then, each night before falling off to sleep, I did it again. It was much harder to do than I thought. After a while, the mornings came back with their usual rush, and I was up and out before realizing I was a thinking creature capable of gratitude. But the evening ritual stayed. Before long it became automatic for me to get into bed and talk to God about everything for which I was grateful. Interestingly, I still started and ended every prayer with the same ritual I learned in second-grade catechism. Praying nightly helped me keep my head out of my own ass (I'm sure the catechism teacher put it differently), and it helped me stay focused on how wonderful life can be when we want to do the work to be at peace. Many times during the day, I would forget this, but I always came back to it at night in prayer.

"Martha, I think of all the winters when you stand there enduring the bitter cold, the snow, the sleet, the darkness. Everything around you looks brown and bleak. The ground is hard at your feet and the sun's love is so distant that we can barely feel its warmth. Yet you persevere. You go through that every winter, yet you never moan about it; you just face it and then you bloom. You know I noticed the harder your winter, the bigger you blossom come spring?"

✾ ✾ ✾

CHRISTMASTIME AROUND OUR HOUSE was always big—I mean really big. I decorated every corner of the house, and if I missed a corner, one of the kids would let me know. It was great how they all had their favorite decorations and looked forward to my putting them up. Rich and I battled often about the excess and the amount of storage space it took up. Barbara appreciated my commitment to Christmas and just bought me more and more decorations. It was a time of love and fantasy in the house, and I worked hard year after year to create memories for everyone.

"Mom, lets decorate Martha," Billy suggested.

"Shit, why didn't I think of that? I have those oversized Christmas balls I was going to use over the staircase. We can use those."

Billy and I bundled up and made our way out the door to Martha. I spent a lot of time close to her in the other seasons, but winter blew so hard in our neck of the woods, I rarely got too close in the winter months.

I took the balls, threaded them each with a long hook, and then handed half to Billy. He went to one side of her bare skirt, and I walked around to the other, reaching out to place the first ball on her naked vine, when suddenly a sharp object cut me.

"WTF, Martha?" I yelled, pulling my hand back and bringing my bleeding fingertips to my mouth.

Billy came running over. "Mom?"

"Look, Martha is covered in tiny thorns. You can barely see them, but she is covered in them," I said as my fingers throbbed.

Billy laughed. "You have to admit, it's kind of funny. She got you good."

"What did I ever do to her? Martha, what did I ever do to you?" I yelled up at her. Actually, I was happy. Martha was so beautiful and soft, delicate and kind, but she was no wuss. She was a lady.

Billy did his best to toss each ball into her skirt. Most of the hooks grabbed on somewhere, leaving her beautifully decorated for the holiday season. We knew there was no way those balls were ever coming down, which made us laugh, thinking of future residents who would be surprised come winter.

🌱 🌱 🌱

IN NO TIME, the holidays were upon us, so I wrote a wish about wanting to gift someone the intangible. I shared it with many, including Leeza, and she asked if she could read it on her radio show, *Hollywood Confidential*. I was very touched.

> *I see the lights outside eager homes. I hear the music play throughout department stores, and there is an excitement on the children's faces that reminds us another year has passed. It is the holiday season once more. A time to celebrate, to express love and kindness.... Our country is at war. Politicians launch battles against one another. And just days ago, mothers and fathers shopping for holiday gifts lost their lives in a Nebraska mall, for some of America's youth are so troubled they find solace in violence. These tragedies I speak of do not remove my holiday spirit, they guide it. They give me a vision of what I should celebrate, how I should love, and what to share. As I inscribe this wish, I know I could address it to most, for life's walk challenges us all. It is the holidays. I have been programmed to give you something I can wrap, something with a bow, but my heart searches elsewhere. I want to give you love, but I do not know how to wrap it. I want to give you respect, but could not find a box big enough. I want to give you my trust, but I do not think the mail carrier could carry it all.... I wish for you those things you cannot touch. I wish you freedom from anxieties, loneliness, and pains of the heart. I wish you the miracles gone unseen as roses blossom in backyards, winter becomes spring again and again, and the sun rises to warm you each and every morning.... If this holiday season I could give you anything, I would wrap your fears, your tears and hold them far from your reach. I*

would give you enough loyalty to erase your betrayals and any
sadness.... This holiday season I will wrap you a gift, but "I love
you" is what I mean to give. For you, I wish the intangible.

The station received great feedback, so Leeza started reading a wish at the end of each show. As the holidays passed and the dread of winter raged on, we were receiving more and more positive feedback from the wishes. A sweet woman from Canada who had recently lost a child wrote a beautiful thank-you. One woman printed one out and held it in the operating room while her son underwent brain surgery; a mom read one to her daughter during her recovery at a drug and alcohol treatment center, and another woman wrote in that she had read one at her daughter's wedding. People wrote in who were mourning a loss, and people who just wanted to say thank you. It was wonderful to watch the wishes touch the lives of others who were experiencing emotions that we all shared. Wishes gave me the chance to give back.

🌳 🌳 🌳

ONE AFTERNOON, I SAT on the couch making earrings for my friends until it was time to prepare dinner. I was determined to get a chicken in the Crock-Pot early and let it slowly cook all day. I was really trying harder in the kitchen, but no matter what I made, everyone

be perfect. I read the directions for the crockpot the night before and asked the butcher a million questions when buying the chicken. And I was prepared with spices and herbs.

I had potatoes to go along with the chicken, and broccoli for nutrition since I was going to smother the potatoes with salt and butter. Lifting the lid of the Crock-Pot, I could see my beautiful, golden brown chicken cooked to perfection. Juices filled the pot and the herbs and spices added a delicious smell. I found an old rubber baster in the bottom drawer and used it to squirt the chicken juices all over the chicken.

"What the fuck?"

My chicken was now green—and not a light green but a bright four-leaf-clover green from the neck to the legs. And the juices were not much prettier, more of an army shade of green, but one thing for sure, everything was green.

I took a moment to ponder and curse before turning to the baster as my culprit. I removed the bulb off the top, and a combination on green paint and chicken juice oozed all over my hands. Jack was constantly doing art projects and using whatever he found in the house to complete them. I examined my chicken once more and knew there was only one thing to do: boil water for the spaghetti.

"MARTHA, I WISH YOU COULD talk louder, because sometimes I can't hear you. Like right now, I wish you could tell me about accepting love.

"I think many people have trouble allowing others to love them. I don't know why. Is it about not feeling deserving? Is the intimacy too awkward? Is it learned behavior? Is it ego?

"Sometimes those who give the most love are the ones who have the hardest time letting others love them. You know, it can hurt to allow love. Oh, I knew you would argue that one with me. But truly, if we have a lot of pain in our hearts, we build walls as protectors. To let someone love you, you have to drop the wall; but if you drop the wall, you become vulnerable to the pain. I guess there are endless reasons why someone would not allow others to love them, including not even realizing what they're doing. But regardless of the reason, we both know you are never going to be healed and be at peace if you don't allow people to love you. Loving is easy. Allowing ourselves to be loved is the challenge."

"MARTHA, IF I HAD A NIPPLE for every person who needed me, I would be covered in tits." I had found a wonderful woman to help me with the big house, but I still felt pulled in many directions and it felt great. I loved being busy and needed.

Usually January was a dark, cold month that kept us inside. But by this time, I had been walking in the woods for years and was moving through a lot of the stuff that held me down. I was reading good books and practicing yoga regularly. I awoke one morning to find the world outside my window blanketed in snow and temperatures that allowed me the freedom to walk. I walked down the road and picked up a trail in the woods near our home feeling as if I were floating, and then I wrote:

> She arrived in the night when all was silent, gently laying her gifts before us. Fascinated by her work, I ventured out to walk among the splendor. What appeared ordinary the night before—a stone wall, a barren tree, the vestiges of a cornfield—was now a magnificent showpiece, as if Mother Nature were calling, "Wake up!" Everywhere I looked she had placed her love in a soft white covering that twinkled as the morning's sun greeted it. A beauty so true and profound, it was magical, a beauty so alive and picturesque, it felt like I was walking through a landscape. And then, I awoke as she spoke in silence. There was no escaping her embrace. I was not just walking through her landscape, I was part of her landscape. I was there in her masterpiece.... Today she leaves me no choice but to see myself as beautiful in her gifts, but does she not offer us beauty every day? Need she shout to be heard? For you, I wish for you to see yourself beautiful today and every day.

🌳 🌳 🌳

IN EARLY MARCH, Mother Nature treated us to a June day. We all knew it was a fluke, a tease, a gift. So the kids jumped on their bikes, Rich went off to play tennis, and I walked.

I headed to a favorite trail surrounding a reservoir that offered woods, water, and wonderment. A big loop provided clarity of thought if I walked it once, and exercise if I walked it twice. Today, once would be enough. I found a spot down near the water to sit and appreciate the warmth of the sun. It had been a hard winter, and looking around, I could easily see the toll it had taken on my surroundings. Things were pretty bleak, everything brown and bare.

But if you stood quietly, you could find a lost piece of yourself in its truth that you might not have known was missing. There was an excitement in the air, a feeling of hope and gratitude, the promise of birth and creativity, of chance and opportunity. It was amazing to witness the world on the verge of lifelessness, knowing colors and birth would soon take over. Mother Nature didn't waste energy being upset about the hardships of winter. She wasn't hanging on to resentment or anger or wallowing in self-pity being a victim of her suffering. She endured it and then she moved on. She also did not give winter any more time or attention than she gave spring, summer, or fall. She endured a long winter. She respected it, yet gave it no more attention or rights than any of her other seasons.

I understood the gravity of this lesson, because I was starting to think a lot about the difference between being a victim and being a survivor. Mother Nature survived all that she experienced by moving right past it and on to the next. I felt that I was a victim of all the loss in my life, but I wanted to be a survivor of it instead. As I looked around me, I could see that being a victim of the pain, of the past, holds you back from truly being at peace and relishing the moments offered by the present. Only by confronting the pain and releasing it would you ever know true peace. You could stay angry and unforgiving, hold on to resentment and have self-pity, but you would never reach your full potential for peace and happiness. To truly live the gift that we have been given, there must be release.

Of course, I knew I would never stop missing my mother and father, but I no longer wanted their death to be something that was done to me. Like Mother Nature opening up to the love and warmth of spring, I wanted to move forward as a survivor.

Where there once was demise, there now was life. Where the earth once stood still, there now is dancing. Spring had finally arrived with her greatest gift: to remind us, young and old, that all is possible.

🌱 🌱 🌱

I CONTINUED TO WRITE WISHES. I sent them to friends and my sisters and Rich, and I bored the children with them. I ran them by Martha, but she seemed to already know most of what I was saying.

One day when I had the kids at the beach, I watched two boys venture out into the ocean together. One of the two was a little more adventurous and headed right out to meet the waves, ducking under each one that came at him. It did not matter how fast the waves were coming or how big they were, he'd successfully duck under each one. The other boy hung back and continuously got hit and knocked down by the waves, never having enough time to regain his composure before getting hit again. When the two were finished swimming, they emerged from the sea, one boy looking strong and invigorated and the other boy looking exhausted and beaten.

I stored up these little bits of nature's wisdom and would pull them out when I needed them. Since I'd been taking my walks and writing my wishes, I was using a lot of analogies to guide the kids. I talked a lot about what I was learning from nature and in yoga. I knew they were growing tired of listening to me, and they ignored half of what I said, but I was happy if they heard half of what I said. I remembered rolling my eyes and ignoring my father's words while growing up, but now as an adult, I could see how his teachings had taught me much more than I'd thought. My only hope was that I was sharing some of that with my own children.

"Olivia, turn that off. Don't you have homework?" I asked.

Olivia, sprawled across the couch with a bowl of popcorn in her hand, watching some pointless television show, responded, "Nothing is due until Friday."

"Did you talk to your teacher about missing class next week? Don't let it become a problem."

"I will. I will."

"Olivia, pretend you are at the beach standing in the ocean. A big wave is coming at you. If you stand still and wait for it to come to you, it is going to knock you over. However, if you swim out to it, you can calmly duck right underneath it and swim to the other side. Get it? Go towards your problems before they knock you over," I said.

"Mom, you're not Buddha," Billy yelled from the other room.

"Yeah, Mom, you're not Buddha," Olivia chimed back.

CHAPTER 12

The Healing Tree

"**M**artha, I fell! I fell!" I yelled over toward her as I got out of my car from yoga practice. I was thrilled about falling, about finally having the courage to take a risk and let myself fall.

After dropping the kids off at school, I walked one of my favorite paths near the junior high. I loved this path—long and narrow; I could see people coming in both directions. This offered me the opportunity to pee if I ever had to. I loved to pee in the woods from time to time. It was freeing and a tad rebellious, despite having to walk the remainder of the trail in urine-damp sweats. It was a great walk: fresh morning air, the birds singing, and the morning glories trailing everywhere. The kids had all gotten to school on time. Everyone was happy and well fed. Rich was in a good mood. It was simply a sweet, cool morning.

After a quick walk, I ran home and changed into my yoga gear, then I headed to class. All the regulars were there chatting away when I arrived, and the energy felt so alive. I knew I was not the only one having a good morning. It felt so good to walk into a room full of smiling faces I recognized and say hello.

When class began, Julie said we would be working on inversions. I loved inversions, and this morning was no different than any other day for me, except when Julie said it was time to practice our Dolphin headstands. Normally I would go over to the wall for support, but that day, I stayed right where I was in the middle of the room. When it came to inversions, I was a pro at the wall, but I was in the middle of the room without a crutch, and I was frozen. Doing a handstand with no spotter took skill I had not mastered yet. However, I was very capable of doing a headstand. I was just fearful of falling. What if I twisted my neck and could no longer move, or hurt my back and was unable to walk for a month? But what if I fell and just simply rolled out of it?

Julie told us to take our time and move at our own pace. It was a level-one class, so most of the class had moved to the wall, but some yogis remained at their mats in the center of the room. I knew there was nothing—nothing—keeping me back from getting into this pose but fear.

Fear. That big, all-consuming word. It holds as much power as its counterpart, love, when you let it. I was consumed by fear and well aware of it. But I did not feel bad about it, because I felt the world was consumed by fear. Sure, my past experiences and neurotic way of thinking may have made my fear more obvious, but everyone lived with fear.

Sometimes fear felt like a security blanket, as if for some crazy reason, if I were afraid, then nothing horrible would happen. However, I'm talking about day-to-day fear that makes people give in to social pressure or hold back. The lengths people will go through to fit in and not be judged are great. But we are social creatures, pack animals, and there is a human survival trait that is deep inside all of us to be accepted. No one wants to get kicked out of the pack and left to be eaten, which may help explain why we feel certain ways— because fear can be so very limiting and so very painful.

☙ ☙ ☙

FOR DEDICATED YOGIS, sometimes there can be nothing worse or better than walking into class and seeing a substitute teacher. My first experience with this tested me on many different levels. One Monday morning after I attended to all my motherly duties, I grabbed my yoga mat and water bottle and headed over to the studio. The parking lot was full, and I saw some of the regulars walking in. As I entered the studio, I looked around for Julie but did not see her. I took my regular place in the back corner and did some stretching. Then a tall, chiseled woman stood in front of the group and introduced herself. She explained that Julie was not feeling well, so she would be filling in. I was greatly disappointed. I loved listening to Julie's teachings, and I loved being led through her practice.

"Today we are going to do something a little different. I'm going to ask you to dedicate your practice to someone, so let's start with three *oms*," she said.

As we went through the typical class openings and warm-ups, I thought of the innumerable people I would love to dedicate my practice to.

"Please come to the front of your mats, standing to face the front of the room," the instructor said. "Now close your eyes and bring your hands together in Prayer Pose. I want you to think of someone who has hurt you, someone who has caused pain in your life, and dedicate your practice to them."

Immediately, the face of someone I did not want to be thinking about flashed into my head.

"Now we are going to move through the class today sending those people love, forgiving them."

I was pissed off immediately. This was fucking bullshit and not what I wanted to be doing on this Monday morning. Yoga was my escape, my time for me. I held resentment, a lot of it, for the person occupying that space in my mind. I had zero interest in sending any love for the next hour and a half in this person's direction, and I was not the only one who seemed bothered by this class exercise.

"What if the person who hurt you is not asking for forgiveness or is not worthy of forgiveness?" asked the yogi front and center.

"Everyone is worthy of forgiveness, because you are worthy of being free from the pain that holding anger brings you."

She continued talking a lot about the harm we do to ourselves when we do not forgive. She spoke about forgiveness being the key to unlocking the anger we hold inside. Throughout the class, as she led us from pose to pose, she would ask us to think of that person again and send love and then more love.

When class was over, I did not feel released of any anger, nor was I feeling peaceful, as I usually felt upon leaving class. I was annoyed and pissy and had to muster up all the maturity I could to whisper a thank-you as I walked out the door.

I walked that day and contemplated the power of forgiveness versus holding on to anger. I understood what the teacher was trying to say. We had all heard numerous times about the negative effects resentment and anger can have on one's soul. All I could do was give it time and try.

I was surprised that the man who had killed my parents had not come to my mind that day in yoga. In the past, he would have been the first, maybe the only one, to come to mind. I did not hold compassion for him, but I did not hold anger either. He was simply no longer a part of my story.

I contemplated anger and sat in thought with this force that rules so much of the living world. Lost for answers, I called on Anger herself to sit with me. She came willingly, much smaller in size than I expected and almost frail in appearance. She sat directly across from me, staring through me. Her intimidation reached for my soul. My heart pounded; my palms sweated. It is hard to confront anger; it takes courage and risk, but I was determined.

"Anger, why, why do you come into our lives and rob us of ourselves?"

She stared and stared, offering no answers, as if unaware of her tremendous devastation. I had come this far; she would not scare me away this time. So I stared back. Surprisingly, I saw tears well up in her eyes. I did not move, but I repeated myself.

"Why, Anger? Why do you come into our lives and rob us of ourselves?"

Now the tears flowed, and the faster they came, the more lost I felt as to how to respond to this force. I spoke slowly, more frightened than I have ever been in my life.

"Anger, I love you."

With that she broke. She wept and wept with her own need to be understood, not feared, her own need for respect.

For you, I wish an understanding of anger.

AS I WALKED MY WALKS, I knew there was so much more to witness than just beauty; there was a handbook to living a life of peace and joy. Nature had taught me so many lessons, but I most loved what she had taught me about forgiveness. All winter long, the ground was hard, the air bitter cold, and the sun distant, but the moment it all softened and asked for forgiveness, she embraced the love and blossomed in an array of color and smells. I understood that forgiveness came from a place of compassion and maturity, sidelining the ego and opening the possibility to bloom.

I once read, "Saying you're sorry does not always mean you are wrong. It means you value the relationship more than the need to be right." I liked that a lot. If we are asked for forgiveness and we are unable to move past it, it's time for self-reflection and personal growth. Maybe there are some things that are unforgivable, but not many. You can choose not to be around people whom you feel are unhealthy to be around, but holding them in anger hurts everyone.

I had offended the person who occupied my mind in class, and they had offended me. However, I had taken responsibility for my part in the situation, never mentioning my hurt feelings, and I had offered a wholehearted apology. When I was not forgiven, I ruminated about it on some of my walks. I thought bad thoughts about the person and analyzed all of the person's misgivings, and I wrote about them. Even though I knew holding on to that anger only hurt me, I could not let it go. The person had dismissed me out of hand. In fact, this person probably would be shocked if they had any idea how much I thought about their dismissal of me. But I had a lot of time alone and a lot of time to think. I found that when I was busy and happy with my life, I didn't think twice about this person.

I realized that forgiveness is much easier to give when we are happy. I was able to release the hurt and anger only when I took responsibility for my actions. I thought hard about the person's perspective and owned up to my end of it in my head. Confronting it allowed me to move past it. I also realized that not being forgiven made me feel terrible about myself, I questioned if I were worthy, etc. But that had nothing to do with the other person; that was all me not loving and respecting myself to understand and forgive myself. I was mad at this person for making me feel a certain way; however, it was me who was giving them the power, and truly they probably didn't care or think about me nearly enough to give a damn.

I assume all of us have a person or two who don't make our holiday gift list. Being a person who is sensitive and may be over-sensitive, I gave other people's criticism of me more attention than it deserved. But you have to know your own head. I wrote a wish once about always checking the weather before going out for a picnic, so always check your head before responding to insult or injury, to limit the drama. It is just as important to bring an umbrella to a picnic on an especially sunny day as it is to remind yourself not to react to people if you were kept up all night by the neighbor's howling dog. Recognize you are exhausted and probably angry. Know what you are bringing to the situation. Someone may throw a stone at you, but that stone can feel like a boulder because of your perception, which only makes things worse for yourself.

It is actually very egocentric to be too sensitive. We can't use our emotions to interpret other people's behaviors; it is not always about us. Many times I have felt foolish when I thought someone was upset with me because of the way he or she was acting, and I then realized the person's behavior had nothing to do with me.

🌳 🌳 🌳

MANY TIMES I WALKED in the glory of nature's white wonderland, but today she appeared beaten down by the elements: her trees were bare, her leaves brown, her animals hibernating. Everything about her was different. She felt bitter against my skin, and she smelled empty. I looked at the trees I called my friends: they looked cold and sad. I wanted to lift them from their roots and bring them home to offer them shelter and warmth.

Trusting that Mother Nature always had wisdom to share, I searched for inspiration. And then I found it: mountains and acres of land, and a windmill I had never seen before, because leaves had obscured my view. I took that as my lesson of the day. Once nature stripped herself of her beauty, you could see things you could not see before. At the end of her cycle she offered clarity. I thought about the quotes, books, and other writings by people who at the end of their life had offered clarity. I knew that all the silly stuff that I let dominate my life would all seem useless and ridiculous one day.

Why do we continue to live with fear and anger? We focus on hurt and pain, resentments and betrayal, even when we know in the end we will recognize its irrelevance.

I saw a fallen acorn lying on the side of the road and picked it up, placing it in my pocket. I would hold on to it and try to remind myself of what I already knew. One day I too will be in the winter of my life. My priorities will change, and I will see things differently. I will regret all the worrying; I will become more compassionate, and I will be upset with myself for not having the courage to live life more freely. I would try to convince my children and grandchildren to learn from my wisdom, but they would have to hold on to most of their stuff so they would have something to reflect on in the winter of their life.

It all seemed so silly, to see it coming yet not be able to redirect it.

❦ ❦ ❦

WHEN SPRING RETURNED, a wave of energy swept through the house, giving us all new direction and hope. Martha starting getting dressed again, baby rabbits scattered from bush to bush, and the birds returned from their trip down South.

Finally, I was able to start walking outside again, and now I walked with a new purpose. I walked with open eyes and an open heart and mind. I observed caterpillars crawling across the ground, listened to every locust I could hear chirp, and touched the different types of moss creeping up the trees.

I studied how Mother Nature's local creeks and river flowed home and watched as debris altered or stilled their mission. I thought about my mission and what debris I was allowing to get in my way: anger, resentment, being oversensitive, fearing the unknown. Alone in my own thoughts so much of the time, I had the clarity to see beauty in front of me that was always there: the way the moon waned and waxed, the twinkle in the stars, the sound of a warm breeze. It does not just happen overnight; it's not like one day you are full of fear and sorrow and insecurities and then the next day you are all better. It is a gradual process of letting go and letting in. Eventually, the balance starts to tip from judgment and fear and pain to compassion and love and gratitude. Slowly, over time, you find yourself working with positive thoughts. You begin to understand and forgive yourself; you accept others for who they are and not who you think they should be. You slowly shift toward love and away from negative ugly energy.

I was getting much better at this, but I knew I was not truly living the life I had been given. I allowed a level of anxiety and neurosis as a result of my past, but that just kept me a victim. I could see my anxiety play out much more clearly. We did have that Red Tent party for Olivia, and it was everything I wanted it to be. But, of course, we had drama surrounding her first period. She was late, the last of her friends to get her period, so I brought her in for test. The doctor did an ultrasound and said Olivia needed a procedure to open a blockage that was preventing her period from flowing. She sent us home with a procedure date and some hormones. About forty-eight hours later, at three in the morning Olivia woke up bleeding and cramping. I panicked and rushed her out the door wrapped in a blanket. We drove down dark, snowy roads to get to the hospital for them to run more tests and tell us Olivia had her period. But when I really realized how stifling my anxiety had become was when I was in Los Angeles for Olivia's Red Tent party and Sheila and I went to a lecture. All the kids were with me, so I left them at Sheila's house with her sitter while Sheila and I attended the lecture. The kids were delighted to have time with Sheila's four children. While we were at the event, Sheila's phone glowed, letting us know a call was trying to come through. I saw Sheila reach down, look at the number, and then go on listening to the speaker.

"Who was it?" I whispered.

"Home," she replied.

"Aren't you going to call back and see what's wrong?" Immediately my mind went into overdrive: someone had fallen, someone choked, there's a problem.

"They are fine. I will call at intermission. Shhh."

I excused myself and went to the bathroom and called Sheila's house. She was right; they just wanted to know if they could order pizza. When I returned to my seat I looked at Sheila, one of the best mothers I know, involved in her children's lives in all ways, intently listening to the speaker. I was so envious.

I knew releasing this anxiety, the neurosis I allowed and accepted, would be my hardest challenge. And I knew the accident was not the cause of my neurotic thinking; the accident just fed it and fed it well. My neurotic thinking was just how my always-working-overtime mind worked. But now I realized I had power over those thoughts if I had the strength and courage to exercise it. Now I knew I could change my thoughts and change my life. When living in Los Angeles I had found happiness and release through the love of others. But I never wanted to feel the pain and loneliness I felt that first year in Connecticut ever again. I had worked through a lot, and I knew that walking around worrying was a waste of the beautiful life I had been given, but could I let it go?

🌳 🌳 🌳

I WALKED AND I THOUGHT and I wrote, and then Leeza called telling me she had someone interested in working with us on a wishes book. When she had suggested earlier that I print the wishes, I insisted she and Barbara be a part of it since the wishes would not be what they were without the two of them. Before long we were doing phone interviews with publishers.

Life pushed on, and I continued getting to yoga class, enjoying the people and practice. My practice remained very challenging, and I still got frustrated with myself, which was extremely anti-yoga. A major goal of the practice was to let yourself be wherever you needed to be at that moment, to love yourself and not compare yourself to the other yogis. One's ego had little place in a yoga studio—or at least mine did. In one evening class, when Julie asked each of us to come to the foot of our mats, I was thinking about Mother Nature and if she had an ego.

The ego always seemed to be the part of the personality that landed a person in trouble, the bad child in an otherwise prudent, upstanding family. I knew my ego had led me to behaviors and thoughts that my heart did not agree with. Yet it was my ego that pushed me the hardest, as if it were the only part of my personality that thrived on risk and living on the edge. Mother Nature had to have an ego; she certainly got grouchy plenty—and sometimes outright wicked with her tornados and hurricanes.

"Tricia, Tricia, you okay?" Julie said softly as she walked past me on my mat.

"Yes, yes, I'm fine," I said, returning my thoughts to the room. I looked around and saw the class in Tree Pose. Without hesitation or patience, I went into the pose and fell right out of it. Julie spoke again from the front of the room.

"Root your right leg into the ground and feel strong before lifting up the left leg.

Get centered, focus ahead of you."

I spotted a small piece of something about two feet in front of me on the floor and focused all of my attention on it. Then, feeling my right leg strong against my mat, I lifted my left leg and planted it firmly on the inside of my right thigh. I held the pose. Just as I was going to lift my arms to the sky, from the corner of my eye I saw a woman in front of me fall out of her pose, and I went down.

Frustrated, I began to give it another try, but Julie moved the class on to another posture.

"Okay, Martha," I said to her as I got out of the car from class, "I get it—mind your own business, keep your thoughts on your own mat. But what if it is more about compassion? She went down and I felt bad, so I went down too. Oh, I know what you are thinking: 'Maybe it is more about not feeling confident enough to be doing better than someone else.' You know, we are not supposed to compare ourselves at all to the other yogis. Ugh, I remember being in my twenties, working for this small family-owned typewriter company. Every so often, we would have a contest to see who could set up the most appointments in one morning. I would always be winning, but then I felt bad because there was a young man in the group I didn't want to outshine. So I would slow down.

"Martha, what the fuck? How ridiculous. You know I was raised with only sisters so it wasn't that I was treated differently, growing up in a family where the sons are treated like kings. I was much older when the epiphany hit me that males were thought of and treated as the superior sex. It was like a child born into a minority family who one day realizes that something as simple and insignificant as the color of her skin would determine so much of her life. So, since I had a vagina, I couldn't win the sales contest. It just didn't feel right. I wonder how many women shared my pathetic insecurities at that time in history. I hope few. Things have changed for women since I was young, but not enough."

I collected some things from the car and headed toward the house. "Goodnight,

Martha. Sleep well. Wait, do you sleep?"

🌳 🌳 🌳

FIRST MY CELL PHONE RANG, but I missed it. Then the house phone rang. It rang as it had many times before. This time it was Rich's voice.

"Tricia, there has been an accident."

Right after my parents' accident, I had felt relief for about ten minutes, as if I thought that I was now safe from anything else bad happening, as if life was fair and I had already gotten my share of bad things. Then I realized life is not fair, and I braced for the next tragedy.

Now I'm petrified because I know how bad it can be.

"Billy was jumping around in the woods, and a tree fell on him. We are waiting for an ambu—"

I hung up on him midsentence.

My thoughts began to swirl. There it was, life laughing and throwing me right to the ground for being so foolish to think I could ever trust it. I began to pace; I did not know what to do, so I called Rich's sister, Dorothy. "Can you call Rich and make sure Billy is okay? I'm freaking out and don't want to hear what he says. Can you make sure he's okay?"

I called Liz and Barbara but reached their voicemails. Dorothy called me back and assured me it would all be okay and she would talk to Rich again once he got to the hospital.

"Should I go now?" I asked.

"Let's wait and see what the doctor says."

I walked around my bedroom in circles before getting the courage to call Rich back.

"What did the doctor say? Can I talk to Billy?"

"Tricia, they are transferring him to another hospital. They think there may be swelling and/or bleeding in his brain, and they are not equipped to handle it here. I think you need to drive up. Can you handle the drive by yourself? It's about three hours from home."

I ran out of the house, taking nothing but a barely charged cellphone. I looked at Martha standing so tall and strong and just whispered, "Help me."

The drive lasted forever. My cellphone died before I crossed the Connecticut–Massachusetts state line. By the time I made it over the Vermont state line it would not have mattered, because the roads I traveled were so remote I do not think cell service could have reached me. The only thing that saved me that night driving on those dark roads was my Sirius radio. I went back and forth between music and listening to my thoughts, controlling my thoughts, changing my thoughts.

Tricia, he is going to be fine. Tricia, not everything ends in tragedy. Tricia, he is going to be fine. Dear God, please, please, please let him be fine. Tricia, calm down.

The hospital came into view from a distance away. An excellent medical hospital connected to one of the country's top schools in the middle of nowhere. Thank you, God.

I was not thinking how worried everyone would be that I had been unavailable for last three hours driving alone, but as I walked through the emergency doors, Rich met me and handed me his cell phone.

"It's Barbara. She's worried sick not to be able to reach you."

I took the phone and said hello as I followed Rich back to see Billy. As we came around the corner, I saw his swollen face being held up by his neck brace and heard the nurse say, "I'm going to give him some morphine now."

I turned around and headed out the door.

"Tricia, get in there," Barbara said.

"Yes, yes, stop running. He's going to be okay," I muttered.

Within moments I collected myself, making sure I appeared calm and strong for Bobby's sake. Rich explained to me that he and his friend had been walking through the woods as the boys ran ahead on the trail. Rich heard a bloodcurdling scream from Bobby, so the men ran. Billy was lying on the ground unconscious with a tree lying across his chest. Rich and his friend lifted the tree off of him. The tree was so heavy, Rich's watch band split open from Rich's wrist expanding. His friend took Bobby and ran for help. Rich stayed with Billy as he bled from his nose and mouth, unconscious. No one saw him have a seizure, but when Bobby was asked what had happened, he said Billy's body was "shaking real bad." Apparently a tree had fallen across another tree. Billy ran and jumped up to do a pull-up on the fallen tree, pulling it right down on him. As Rich spoke, I felt ashamed imagining the terror he must have felt holding Billy, unconscious and bleeding, all alone in the forest. And then I remembered hanging up on him.

I sat holding Bobby next to Billy, who remained still and silent. Bobby was calm, playing a game on Rich's phone, when all of a sudden Billy began vomiting dark blood all over the floor. Bobby jumped off my lap and threw open the curtain yelling, "Call 911!"

The nurse ran in, helping Billy and explaining to us that he had swallowed a lot of blood and the morphine was making him sick.

It was close to midnight and Bobby had been through too much in one day for his little life. Rich and I agreed that I would take him to the local hotel and wait there for Billy's test results to come back. Those first twelve hours would be very telling. Of course, my support system kicked in, and I was on the phone most of the night—with my sister Liz and Rich's family and Barbara—keeping everyone updated.

I have had long nights before, and this one was no different. Then somewhere in the middle of the night, we were informed that there was no bleeding or swelling. Billy had suffered a major concussion and would need surgery to fix his nose, which was now planted deep in his face.

Days after the surgery, I was looking at Martha with a whole new respect—how dangerous and powerful a tree could be. I was pissed.

"Martha, what the fuck? One of your tree friends is a real asshole."

The next few weeks were not easy, but soon Billy was able to return to school. Then the jokes started, like, "If a tree falls in the woods and Billy's face is not there to catch it, did it still fall?"

🌱 🌱 🌱

"Watch this, Martha," I said, standing tall on my right leg as I pulled my left leg up and rested my foot on my inner thigh, but I fell out of it as I heard the door open behind me. Billy and Bobby walked out of the garage with a soccer ball, heading to the backyard.

"Why are you so obsessed with that pose?" Billy asked.

He walked over to me and Martha with Bobby on his heels, and got into Tree Pose without even the use of his hands, and then Bobby followed. They both stood there as if it were as easy as walking. Then they headed off to the backyard.

Over the past few weeks, I ended each walk facing Martha, trying to triumph at Tree Pose. I envisioned her roots beneath the ground running across the yard, coming out of the dirt, and wrapping themselves around my standing leg to anchor me into the ground. This seemed to help, and I was able to hold the pose for what felt like minutes but was only seconds. Martha knew best how much it bothered me—and still does. It haunts me, this thing, this Tree Pose thing I have been trying to master much of my adult life. And by adult life, I mean the last couple of years. Up until then, I think I was still growing up—interesting, the sheer reality that I did not know I was not being a grown-up until I became one. Although I love the independence that being a grown-up offers me—the freedom of not needing others' approval, the absence of wanting to share every woe and success with everyone I know, I had to admit I missed some parts of it.

The funny thing about this pose I've been trying to master is that it sums up my life. To achieve it, you must be strong, but not too strong. You must stay focused without getting into your head too much. You must be soft but, of course, never too soft, and you must be open while being grounded. Martha knows; it's a simple Tree Pose. Some days I hit it, and I'm filled with pride, as if my ability to remain in the pose is a direct reflection of my mindset and how together I am. Other days, I fall out of it again and again, and I get really down on myself for not being more centered as a person and not having my shit together.

I have learned that the best way to hit this pose is to stay focused, look straight ahead, and not worry about what's happening on other people's mats. However, no matter how hard I try, I can see them all out of the corners of my eyes. So, can I hit this pose? Am I focused, strong, soft, and open? Does my life have balance? Why am I so challenged by this simple balancing pose of standing on one leg while placing the other on my thigh?

🌱 🌱 🌱

SEASONS CHANGED. I had good friends, and I had learned to be alone without being lonely. Actually, I had learned to love being alone. The kids were flourishing and happy. I was happy. We settled deeper into our lives in Avon. All was good. Summer ended and a new school year began, and then Rich's company closed down his whole department.

We were moving again.

"Martha, the idea of moving again doesn't upset me. I have done what I needed to do before leaving Connecticut, and I'm ready to try something new. A company in the Seattle area hired Rich, and I'm excited to get back to the West Coast. I have never spent time in the Pacific Northwest and am looking forward to getting to know the area. The kids will have a much more difficult time with this move, since they are older and their friends mean more to them. Olivia hates the idea of us all being across the country from her college. Yet everyone knows that Daddy needs a job, and we are in this together.

We did the same drill: Rich went out to Washington and settled in while I stayed back with the kids as they finished out the school year. One day while I was thinking about how hard those first years had been for me in Avon, Bobby came running into my room delighted with himself.

"Mommy, Mommy! Look, I picked you a beautiful flower!" He reached out his hand, opening his tightly gripped fingers, and laid a freshly picked dandelion beside me.

Life is beautiful.

THE KIDS WERE HAVING a great school year, and we were beginning to look at colleges for Olivia. The thought of not having all four of my children under my roof confirmed a decision I had made many years ago.

"Tricia, you can't make the kids live near you forever," Rich said.

"Yes, I can. I've told them they are not allowed to move away, so they know they can't leave. In the old days, people lived next door to their families forever." I wasn't worried about Olivia and Bobby; I knew they would always stay close by. But Billy and Jack were much more independent.

"You are crazy," Rich said. "I'm just saying you can't hold on to them forever."

"Watch me."

I walked out the side door connecting the kitchen to the garage and then out to

Martha. "Watch me, Martha, I will hold on to them forever."

I felt like she got it; she understood that in my sarcasm was my truth. I did not need them living under my roof, but I had every intention of spending the rest of my life with them all nearby. Letting them have their own life stuff was overrated.

I tightened every muscle down my midline and breathed deeply, pressing my foot harder against my leg as I raised both my arms high into the sky. I was doing it and it felt invigorating.

"Look, Martha, Tree Pose. I'm doing it!"

I could feel her smile.

I stood there for as long as I wanted and then, with control, I let down my foot to the ground. I decided not to push my luck and try the other side; I just rejoiced in my accomplishments and headed down the driveway for my daily dose of inspiration.

She wished to shower her children in splendor, so she created a never-ending sky, a sunset high, stars and the moon, waterways vast and salty, long and narrow. She created hills, valleys, forests thick in green, and flowers of all shapes and sizes. Exhausted, she paused, fearing her work lacked luster. In her frustration, she created thunderstorms, droughts, and landslides. She paused again, this time met with clarity. Love she missed, so love she gifted. In a moment, the sun radiated heat; the stars began to twinkle; the moon waned and waxed. The sky produced rainbows, sunsets, and sunrises; the rivers flowed and the ocean roared. Flowers burst with scent, trees danced in color.

Love, an emotion to heal and nurture, to be shared by all with all. With it you have everything; without it you have nothing. For you, I wish love.

🌳 🌳 🌳

MY MIND WAS OPENING UP to a new way of thinking. Had it been shown to me before and I just missed it? Or did I need this time alone in a place of utter despair to find it? The more I cleared my mind, the more I was able to decipher Mother Nature's language, and the more I could hear God speaking to me. I had gone to church numerous times, I had read religious writings, but alone in nature, I could not deny the possibility of God. Every day, I set out for a walk with new ambition and came home with new hope. I was so inspired by the beauty and wisdom that the anger and despair that had once torn at my heart was gone. Conveying the gifts that nature offered me through wishes felt like my spiritual purpose, and for the first time in my life, I felt connected to God.

It was strange to me, the way the wishes would come into my head. I was not a writer or a poet in any way. My spelling was dreadful and my grammar worse. Yet, as I walked, words just flowed through my mind and then onto paper. I realized that I had never been still or quiet long enough in my life to hear God speak to me. I sat through countless religious classes and sermons smiling while my mind had me at the playground or capturing a unicorn.

I wrote numerous wishes and paused when I finished the ninety-ninth. It meant a lot to me that the hundredth wish be special, but I was at a loss. Would I write it for Barbara, since she was the reason I started writing wishes? Or would I write it for Leeza for all her encouragement in moving them forward? Would I write it to Rich as a love letter, or do I write it to the wishes themselves? And what about Martha and the children? I had no idea what I was going to write, so I just let it go and tried to stay open.

Then one night, a wish came into my head that felt like it was written for everyone, a piece of truth and love for all.

A hundred breaths ago, I stood naked in faith at the ocean's edge waiting for a message in a bottle to lead me. You washed upon my shores with a deepness in your eyes so trusting, I knew I was born loving you. This love was unexpected and sweet, just ours to share. When grief made it too hard to breathe, you restored my breath....

A hundred breaths ago, I stood naked in wisdom at the ocean's edge, unaware of my need for you. You came as a teacher converting me into a student of life in search of more. With you, I found humility and gratitude; I confronted weakness and inse-curities. The strength and courage that was always there inside of me, you showed me....

A hundred breaths ago, I stood naked in passion at the ocean's edge, and you took my breath away with yours. My

dreams became your dreams, as yours became mine. You shel-
tered me and protected me. In my darkness you survived me
with your stillness, always standing right where I left you when
the lightness returned.

In a hundred breaths, in every breath, I wish for you all my
love, all my life.

🌱 🌱 🌱

"MARTHA, DO YOU THINK people can be at peace without God in their lives? I do. However, I don't think you can be at peace without grati-tude and love."

God is love and gratitude.

"I knew you were going to say that. And you're right."

I realized I had learned to accept responsibility for myself, to not be needy and not expect others to fix my pain. I had learned to be alone and not be lonely, to not judge and to be open-minded and more accepting. I had learned to find happiness after being so sad. But the greatest lesson of all: I knew that just like Mother Nature repeating her daily rituals and four seasons, I would slip and contin-uously need to bring myself back to a place of love. I would forget my manners and judge, I would ruminate about silly stuff, and I would get easily offended. There would be days I would be unappre-ciative and have self-pity. And days I'd lose my confidence and need reminding of the power I had inside of me for me. I knew all of this would come around again; that was the nature of life. But it would be up to me to catch myself and then get myself back on track.

🌱 🌱 🌱

I LOOKED AT THE CLOCK and noticed it was ten past eleven, so Olivia was late. Just as I reached for my phone to call her, the front door opened.

"I'm home. Sorry I'm late, but the line at the drive-through McDonald's took forever," she said as she entered my room, shoving a large fry into her mouth.

"Did you have fun?" I asked

"Yes but, Mom, ugh."

"What?"

"I was standing there, and I noticed a guy a couple years older than me who I knew was over at the house once with Amy when she tutored Jack. Remember Amy from when we first moved in, who helped Jack with math or something?"

"And you. Of course I do."

"Well, when I introduced myself, do you know what he asked me?"

"I have no idea. What did he ask you?"

"He said, 'Hey, aren't you that girl whose mom talks to trees?'"

"Well, I don't talk to *trees*, just a tree. I may be a little crazy, but I haven't lost my mind. Did you correct him?"

"Mom!"

"Well, at least he remembered you," I yelled to her as she headed out of my bedroom.

❦ ❦ ❦

IT WAS THAT TIME AGAIN, when we packed up the house, changed our address, and said our goodbyes. But this move was different. I was sad to leave, but I felt my time in Avon was fulfilled. The one I would have the most trouble saying goodbye to was the one I could not text or phone or have come visit me, the one who had stood still for me so I could find my way and see all the beauty of my world. Martha.

Every time I looked at her in the months and weeks before our departure, I cried. We had been through so much together, and I was beyond grateful. Yet I noticed myself looking for reasons to get mad. In the mornings when I was running late for carpool, I would feel her disapproving look, and once I actually yelled at her for being judgmental.

On another occasion, I just lost it. I was exhausted and completely stressed out about getting the house prepared, the kids had a million things going on, and when I walked outside the house to go get the mail, it felt like Martha was looking at me saying, "Calm down for fuck's sake." She wasn't much of a curser, so I knew she was mad. I shot a look back and replied, "What do you know about moving? You have stood in the same goddamn place for the last 100 years, so don't give me your attitude."

I was fighting with a tree!

Nevertheless, my heart broke thinking of saying goodbye to her. I couldn't hug her or send her gifts; I couldn't call her like I could Terese or Barbara—I just had to say goodbye. She had offered me so much safety and love. Everyone who knew me knew about Martha.

So I decided to get her a friend. What was so wonderful was that when I told Rich about my idea, he spent time with me in the yard deciding where we would plant her friend. I had already known the kids loved Martha, but now I knew Rich loved her too.

And I knew exactly what tree I would buy her.

Once when Barbara had visited, I was excited to show her the bright purple tree in our neighbor's yard, since purple was her favorite color. We walked the neighborhood, and as we turned the corner to where the beautiful tree was living, all we could see was green. The blossoms were gone and only leaves were left. But something magnificent happened as we got closer. We could see the shape of her leaves, all hearts. What a wonderful tree; she blossomed in purple and then rested in hearts! We named her the Tinkerbell tree and took one of her leaves home with us. I knocked on the neighbor's door and was told she was an Eastern redbud.

This was the type of tree I wanted to give Martha. My plan was to get a tree sometime before we moved, but then something unusual happened. I got a call from my friend Lynn, a wonderful woman I had known all my life, with whom I had recently reconnected.

"Trishy, I know this amazing priest who writes poetry. Do you think you could read his work? Can I bring him by your house tomorrow around 2:00 p.m.?"

Lynn was one of the world's most fantastic people, and I would never say no to her about anything. "Will he bless Martha for me?"

The next day I went to yoga and allowed my yoga girls to giggle at the thought of a priest in my home. They knew I had been raised a good Catholic girl but struggled with my faith. I no longer would just show up and go through the motions. That was disrespectful to the church and to me. So the thought of a priest entering my home was anxiety-provoking, which was part of being a Catholic, the guilt. Of course I would have to tell the priest I had left the church. That was part of me being me.

"Well you don't have to tell him; you can just say you go to St. Anne," Terri offered.

"That wouldn't be any fun. Plus, if I have left the church, I should be able to discuss it. I just wish I had already bought Martha's friend so he could bless the two of them."

"Go get her," Pam said.

"I have the jeep with me. We can go over to the nursery in Simsbury after class," Andrea offered.

So we did just that. Andrea and I drove over to the Simsbury Gardens and picked out the sweetest Eastern redbud tree in the lot and bought her home and placed her right in front of Martha. It was amazing how I immediately felt better about leaving her.

"Martha, we are having a special visitor tomorrow, so be respectful. I have a few things I would like to ask. I mean if everyone had drunk all the wine at the wedding, wasn't it time for everyone to go home?"

The priest showed up at my house and was just perfect. He explained the significance behind the first miracle, and when we spoke of my finding God on my walks and no longer attending mass, he said nothing; he was just happy I found God. He was kind and wise.

I read his poetry, which was full of beauty and passion; I told him about my positive experience writing wishes and offered him publishing advice. And then we walked to the yard. It was then, in that moment, that I felt a little silly about Martha. Lynn, the Father, and I bowed our heads and closed our eyes while he gave the girls a blessing. But his words were so very beautiful, my embarrassment faded.

The next day we planted Tink in the ground. Byron, Barbara and Wolfgang's son, was visiting from Los Angeles, so he and Billy performed a Tink-planting ceremony. It was perfect the way I could get the kids to help me with the yard when I named the tree. I knew if I had said, "Billy, go dig a three-foot hole in the yard and plant this tree," he would have come up with a reason why he could not do that. Yet if I asked to please put Tink in the ground before her roots got damaged, all of the kids would comply, like they would help out if a pet needed them.

We emptied our house and moved into the local hotel for two weeks. This gave me ample time to prepare the house for renters and for us all to say our goodbyes. I realized I was worried about Tink; she was so newly planted, and we would not be there to care for her as she adjusted to her new environment. So the day before we left town, I went to the local nursery. An old man with great deep lines covering his face, reflecting all the time he had spent in the sun, came around the corner, startling me with his rough voice.

"Can I help you?"

"Yes, I just planted a tree in my yard, an Eastern redbud. I am moving tomorrow, so I'm worried for her. I was hoping to get some food to give her the best chance for survival."

"You are moving tomorrow but just planted the tree?"

"Yes."

"It doesn't need anything."

"There is nothing I can give her?" I asked.

He paused and looked at me for a moment, then replied, "Once she roots herself, she will take care of herself."

And there it was. "Once she roots herself in the ground, she will take care of herself." Those words ran through my head a million times that night.

I had done that in Avon; I had rooted myself into the ground and I was now able to take care of myself. Yes, human kindness was invaluable, and it held me until I was strong enough to hold me. Not until I was rooted and able to take care of myself would all the wounds and pain and voids of my heart be able to completely heal. I had done that without even realizing it until now. And I now understood why the sequoias were the tallest in the forest. It was the strength within each individual tree that offered strength to the other; their collective strength allowed them to depend on one another and be the best they could be.

The next morning came with anxious bellies and anticipation. I got up early while the kids were still sleeping and headed to my favorite Starbucks for the last time. I got my latte and headed over to the house. The morning was wonderful: not too hot yet, the birds singing to one another, and the sky a fabulous shade of blue. I sat in Martha's shade as I sipped my coffee, thinking about how miserable I was when I had first arrived in Avon, how young I was in my ability to hold my own, about all the walks and talks, all the tears and fears left at her feet. I thought about learning to be alone without feeling lonely and about how I was now able to make good of the loss I had suffered by helping others. Of all the places I had lived, Avon had been the toughest, but it had taught me the most. It showed me that I was strong, I could take care of myself, and I would be all right; I *was* all right.

I blew a kiss to Tink and then with only a tear in my eye looked

I am left to ponder the profound notion that it all came for a reason, that it was all meant to be, a spiritual harmony so beautiful in sound, I cannot deny its music.

🌳 🌳 🌳

THREE THOUSAND MILES and days later, I left sleeping teenagers in our new home and headed over to a local studio to try out one of their yoga classes. I felt comfortable the moment I walked in the door and loved the bubbly energy of the instructor teaching the class.

After finishing the physical part of our practice, the teacher instructed us to lie in Shavasana, Corpse Pose, when you lie perfectly still and try to empty your mind.

Meditation was hard for me—very hard. I believed so deeply in the human body's caring for itself that I was perplexed about why meditation was difficult to reach. As it's a life-changing, stress- and anxiety-reducing aid for the human mind, one would think nature would offer it up more easily. Since my mind usually worked overtime, this was the hardest part of the yoga class for me, but I soon got increasingly better at it. On a few special days, I got to experience a true Shavasana, being in that place between the conscious and the unconscious that offers a window into the unknown.

This time became sacred to me, when I could achieve it, so I worked hard at making it happen. I found having the perfect physical balance, a much-appreciated caffeine buzz with the nutrition of half a banana, gave me my best chances of making it happen by keeping my mind and body light. If I consumed much more than that, I felt bogged down; less and I felt dizzy.

Lying still on my mat, I let go of the to-do list and went to my spot on the beach, allowing the sun and God's love to shine down on me. I would envision a beam of blue light coming down from the sky straight through my heart, running down to my toes and up to my head. On the few days I felt emotionally depleted, I would hold on to the light and let it rejuvenate me. On other days, I would let the blue light fill me, but then I would send it back out into the world in shades of bright yellow. I would send it to parts of the world I knew were suffering and needing love.

And then on other days, I would use the light to visit Martha. When I felt the warmth of the blue light embrace me like a cocoon, I zoomed myself across the country to my safe place with her. "Dear Martha, you changed your clothes again." I talked to Martha whenever I needed, but I actually felt her while in Shavasana—while in meditation.

I once found myself at Martha's feet, but to my surprise there were my mother and father on the porch and Aaron playing soccer in the backyard. My father read the paper as my mother leaned over the railing watching Aaron. He was so happy running down the yard shooting the ball into the goal. They looked beautiful and peaceful, but it was too much for me. I imagined them away, but they would not go—my unconscious mind overpowered my conscious mind. Again, I tried asking Martha, "Please tell them to go away. Tell them I love them, but I only want to talk to you right now."

They went nowhere and Martha stayed silent.

"I don't want you here right now if that's okay," I said, but none of them would leave. I was so deep in Shavasana, the only part of me in the yoga classroom was my physical body. I tried to wake up without moving, but my mind had me locked in. Then I did something I had never done before. Like a four-year-old child, I ran to Martha's skirt and hid, tucking into a ball with my back pressed up against her. My mind and body caught between two worlds, I could feel tears running down my face.

And then the unthinkable happened.

My yoga teacher bent down and started pressing down on my shoulders as a reminder to release my stress. My mind raced, afraid physical touch would break me and I would start bawling right there in the middle of the room. I tried again to release my mind from the scene and return to the classroom where my mind was, but they kept me right there, locked in their presence. I could see them through Martha's skirt, my mother and my father looking serious and Aaron smiling at me as if I were going to get in trouble. They just stood there waiting for me to come out. More tears fell from my face as my teacher gently pressed my shoulders to the ground. What was she thinking? Did she notice the tears? Did she think they were sweat? Could she sense my turmoil? My mind raced back and forth; I was completely vulnerable to her touch and defeated by their refusal to go. I had no choice but to leave the protection of Martha and confront them.

As I crawled under Martha's skirt, my yoga teacher moved her hands from my shoulders to my forehead, and began brushing her hands down the sides of my face. I knew if I made any sudden moves, I would have a breakdown, so I stayed calm, allowing it all to unfold. My yoga teacher caressed my face as my mind eased me out in the open. My mother and father and Aaron stood there, and without talking, they let me know they were not going away. My father seemed happy with that and walked away. Aaron trailed him, kicking his ball up ahead, but my mother reached to hug me.

I tried to stop her, but I had no control of my own thoughts. She embraced me, as my teacher left my side and headed back to the front of the room. I stayed still until the soft voice of our teacher slowly awakened us, guiding us to an upright position. I remained committed to no outburst, no commotion, yet I wanted to scream, "Does anyone know what just happened?" We closed the practice with one *om* and then bowed *namaste* to one another. I quietly rolled up my mat, avoiding eye contact with everyone, and headed out the door.

The rhythm of her heart soothed you long before you took your first breath of air. Her arms cradled you, her kisses smothered you. She held your hand, tied your shoes, brushed your hair. When you were scared, she reassured you; when you were sad, she comforted you. She knew you better than you knew yourself. She is your mother. Tonight you are asked to say goodbye to her, a quest too grand to comprehend. We are never ready to say goodbye to our mothers regardless of age, for we are all the child looking up into her eyes when it is time to depart. She cannot hold you now; she cannot nurture your bleeding heart or wipe the tears from you swollen eyes. Mother Nature knew we would all have to say goodbye to our mothers one day, and that this departure would redefine our being and leave us hollow inside, so she gifted all of her children with maternal love. Maternal love to share with one another when a mother must go. Your mother has wrapped her arms around many others in times of grief and heartache; now let them wrap their arms around you. Find your mother's love in all who love you. See her eyes twinkle through a baby's smile, feel her wisdom in a friend's devotion. In a field of daisies rest your voice and look to the sky, remember the smell of her skin, the softness in her touch. The way her kiss took away the pain of a scraped knee, the way her voice centered your world. As you feel her so close to you, let the rhythm of her heart soothe you once more and you will come to realize that you started off as one and became two. Now you are one again. This time it is she who lies within you, for she will forever be in your heart. For you, I wish your Eternal Mother.

AS WE ADJUSTED to our new home in the Northwest, I found some paths to walk and got to yoga as much as possible. One morning while finishing up class, I really wanted to be with Martha; however, I had created a problem for myself while visiting Martha during Shavasana. Ever since I had found my mother and father and Aaron in the yard with her, they were always there when I visited her. Of course, having them there was a blessing too grand to explain, but it took an emotional energy that sometimes I did not want to deal with. I had spent more than a decade learning to be lighter and live in gratitude without painful thoughts; sometimes I wanted things to stay light and easy. That day, I just wanted to say hello to Martha and then get out of there and get back to thinking about the grocery list and dinner plans. I just did not feel like ripping it all up. I did not want to live in the past; I wanted to live in the future, the future that I had busted my ass to create.

So I was left with a huge dilemma. If I went to Martha in meditation, my family would be there, and I knew I would not only think of them but also feel them. I had come to a place where these deep emotions were for special times, but not for every day at yoga practice. I thought of the time I had asked Terese if I was the girl who had lost her parents in a car accident, and she had asked me if that was who I wanted to be. At the time, the answer was yes. But that was not who I was. I was not the girl who had lost her mother and father in a car accident and her nephew to an overdose. I was just Tricia—no longer in search, just Tricia.

But what about Martha?

An epiphany hit me, first in my mind and then in my stomach and heart.

"Dear Martha, WTF?"

But she knew what I was going to say; it was probably her doing. It was time to let Martha go, just as I had Terese and Barbara. At the time in my life when I needed them, they appeared as if they had always been there. But now I needed only to love them. Maybe it was time for me to be someone else's Terese or Barbara, maybe it was time for me to help people find their own Martha. Leaving my parents and Aaron with Martha, in the place I found self-love and trust, was perfect. On special occasions, I would visit them. As they'd told me before, "We are not going away," but for today, it was time to let go.

So I lay back on my mat, closed my eyes, and went off into meditation, a deep, powerful meditation. I took myself to a new beach, a beach with pure white sand and turquoise gentle water. I lay at the ocean's edge, feeling the warmth of the sand against my back. I looked to the sun high in the sky and let its love engulf me in a deep, beautiful shade of blue. I embraced the love, feeling it fill me from my toes to the top of my head. Then straight through my heart, I sent all that love back out into the world in a bright shade of yellow with tones of gratitude, peace, and joy.

Namaste.

Connected

I recently visited Martha and Tink in Connecticut. We still own the property where they live, so I knew the residents were away on vacation. It was wonderful to sit not only with Martha but also with Tink. She had obviously rooted herself deep into the ground and was taking care of herself. Her leaves were three times the size they had been when we planted her, big and green and heart-shaped. Although she is just a trinket next to Martha, she has weathered the harsh winter storms of the Northeast during the last few years.

Martha was so grand, so abundant, so wonderful. Her branches were long and strong and as beautiful as ever. Her skirt appeared as if she had made some changes to it; some vegetation I had not noticed before hung long in an array of shades of green. Under her canopy, I could see some very weathered Christmas balls lying on the ground. But most interestingly, her skirt had grown oddly off to the side, looking as if she were sweetly reaching for Tink's hand. The storms had been brutal that winter, and maybe, just maybe, she was trying to comfort her new friend.

Sitting beneath them, I could hear the sounds of the breeze passing through the leaves of all the trees nearby.

After my parents died, I used to pretend that this beautiful sound was them laughing in the trees. I could hear locusts and birds and silence and love. The house in front of me and a neighbor's garage were the only signs of human life; everything else was nature.

I thought a lot about my years living in this home, about the children growing and about my time with Martha. The peace before me was brilliant. There was no war or hatred or judgment or drama or sadness, nothing there under their branches but peace and love.

Maybe everyone is supposed to have a tree friend, but they just don't know it. I know I have a big imagination, but I also know what I feel, and when sitting with Martha and Tink, I feel love and peace and security. I allowed myself to feel it, and it is there.

I wish for you to find your tree. She or he is out there waiting for you to look up.

Acknowledgments

This book has been a process and has taken many years to complete. Not because I was writing and rewriting all these years, but because I needed to live life for those many years to arrive at a place where I felt the book was finished. I am in gratitude to so many for being part of my life.

My deepest gratitude is for my best friend and loving husband, Richard LaVoice. Thank you for loving me so well. I love sharing my life with you.

I share my heart with my incredible, courageous sister Elizabeth and devoted, sweet sister Virginia. Also with their amazing children, David, Julie, and Tricia, Aaron's siblings, who through their hardships stay devoted to positive thoughts and love. And with our wonderful Vanessa.

A huge thank-you to my wonderful LaVoice family, Don, Betty, Donna, Pete, Dorothy, David, Corrie, Eileen, and the children, who took me in and loved me like kin from day one.

Over the course of my life, so many friends have come and most have stayed. Their love and support humble me. With deep love and appreciation, I thank my Long Beach family, Dan, Bobbie, Kristan, and Lauren; my NYC friends, Carol, Susan, and Hope; my Mill Valley coffee clutch, Lisa, Gail, and Carrie; my beautiful circle of love in Los Angeles, Carlene, Sondra, Leeza, Barbara, Muna, Holly, and Nancy; my yoga goddesses from Avon, Julie, Pam, Terri, and Andrea; and my incredible, loyal group of friends from Yardley who have been at my side through it all, Mary, Linda, Donna, Sheila, Amy, Wendy, Becky Leigh Ann, Susan, Lisa, Sally Monica, Jill, Andy, Nicki, and Scott.

A special thank-you to Lynn, Arthur, Jody, Beth, Carrie, Deb, Cheryl, Judy, Kim, and sweet Pam for their constant encouragement.

Another huge thank-you to my sister Elizabeth and beautiful friends Sheila Katerndahl and Leeza Gibbons, who all unwearyingly read every version of this book.

I give gratitude to my intelligent, insightful editors, Allison McCabe, Joni Rodgers, and Jennifer Holder for teaching me how to turn a story into a book. And to Audrey Shepard, who saved me in the end.

A special thank-you to the wonderful CEO of Dupree Miller and Associates, Jan Miller, and President Shannon Marven for their support and vision.

With gratitude, I thank the publishing team at Post Hill Press, with a special thank-you to Billie Brownell for her editorial insight and President Anthony Ziccardi for his witty candor and patience.

My love and loyalty to Barbara Lazaroff and Terese Payne for the maternal love that served as inspiration for this book. You both came into my life at a time when I was so in need of your love. My only explanation was that my mother must have sent you. I love you both and thank you...and Martha too!

To Olivia, Billy, Jack, and Bobby, being your mother has been the greatest gift of my life. You have all grown into such interesting, kind, beautiful people. I can't wait to see what life has in store for all of you. I will always be right there with you (even when you wish I weren't).

Finally, I would like to thank my incredibly talented agent, Lacy Lynch. Lacy, if thank-yous were flowers, I would send you Versailles. It was your belief in me that enabled me to finish and publish this book. I am forever grateful for you.